The Practical Witch's Almanac

2024

Growing Your Craft

Volume XXVII
by Friday Gladheart

PRACTICAL WITCH'S ALMANAC 2024:
GROWING YOUR CRAFT
© 2023 Friday Gladheart
© This edition Microcosm Publishing 2023
First edition
ISBN 978-1648411625

To join the ranks of high-class stores that feature Microcosm titles, talk to your rep: In the U.S., **Como** (Atlantic), **Abraham** (Midwest), **Third Act** (Texas, Oklahoma, Louisiana, Arkansas), and **Imprint** (Pacific). **Turnaround** in Europe, **Manda/UTP** in Canada, **New South** in Australia, and **GPS** in Asia, India, Africa, and South America. We are sold in the gift market by **Faire** and **Emerald.**

For a catalog, write or visit:
Microcosm Publishing
2752 N Williams Ave.
Portland, OR 97227
https://microcosm.pub/PracticalWitch

The content of this almanac is for informational purposes only, and is not intended to diagnose, treat, cure, or prevent any condition or disease.

The data in this almanac is calculated for Central Time. It is easy to convert the data to any time zone with the information on pages 185 and 186.

MICROCOSM · PUBLISHING

About the Publisher

MICROCOSM PUBLISHING is Portland's most diversified publishing house and distributor with a focus on the colorful, authentic, and empowering. Our books and zines have put your power in your hands since 1996, equipping readers to make positive changes in their lives and in the world around them. Microcosm emphasizes skill-building, showing hidden histories, and fostering creativity through challenging conventional publishing wisdom with books and bookettes about DIY skills, food, bicycling, gender, self-care, and social justice. What was once a distro and record label started by Joe Biel in a drafty bedroom was determined to be *Publisher's Weekly's* fastest growing publisher of 2022 and #3 in 2023, now become among the oldest independent publishing houses in Portland, OR and Cleveland, OH. We are a politically moderate, centrist publisher in a world that has inched to the right for the past 80 years.

Global labor conditions are bad, and our roots in industrial Cleveland in the 70s and 80s made us appreciate the need to treat workers right. Therefore, our books are MADE IN THE USA

Did you know that you can buy our books directly from us at sliding scale rates? Support a small, independent publisher and pay less than Amazon's price at **www. Microcosm.Pub**

Growing Your Craft

Have you ever taken one of those social media quizzes to find out what kind of a witch you are? The results help you identify some of the different flavors of witchcraft, and you may resonate with a particular label provided in your quiz results. That's great! It is exciting to find a path with which you feel connected. However, as you navigate your path, you will grow and change. You may feel that you are a "green witch" at one point and later think that the label "hedge witch" suits you better.

Witch labels can help us direct our studies in our favorite areas, but only if we do not allow the labels to hold us back. As you travel your path, you'll notice that your interests and skills may fall outside your adopted label.

This year's *Practical Witch's Almanac* explores diverse topics to enrich your path. Each week has a subject, but these differ from school lessons. There won't be tests, and you are the instructor.

The weekly selections engage you in exploring various topics in the witch's repertoire. When you find a subject particularly interesting, you can expand your knowledge with bonus materials at the official website, PracticalWitch.com/My2024, or listen to The *Practical Witch Talk* podcast on your favorite streaming service. Each week in 2024 features an episode on the topic that appears in your almanac.

Labels are for Potions

In a world of judgment and disguise,
Where labels confine and categorize,
I call upon forces of liberation,
To break free from societal dictation.
For labels, dear ones, are meant for potions,
Not to define our hearts' emotions.
In each soul's essence, a universe unfolds,
A tapestry of stories yet untold.
Embrace the fullness of your being,
With all its complexities, all worth seeing.
For within our hearts, we hold a power,
To rise above labels and to truly flower.
So let it be, this invocation's decree,
That labels are for potions, not you and me.
~Friday Gladheart

January

M	T	W	T	F	S	S
1	2	3	4	5	6	7
8	9	10	⬤11	12	13	14
15	16	17	18	19	20	21
22	23	24	(25)	26	27	28
29	30	31				

February

M	T	W	T	F	S	S
			1	2	3	4
5	6	7	8	⬤9	10	11
12	13	14	15	16	17	18
19	20	21	22	23	(24)	25
26	27	28	29			

May

M	T	W	T	F	S	S
		1	2	3	4	5
6	⬤7	8	9	10	11	12
13	14	15	16	17	18	19
20	21	22	(23)	24	25	26
27	28	29	30	31		

June

M	T	W	T	F	S	S
					1	2
3	4	5	⬤6	7	8	9
10	11	12	13	14	15	16
17	18	19	**20**	(21)	22	23
24	25	26	27	28	29	30

September

M	T	W	T	F	S	S
						1
⬤2	3	4	5	6	7	8
9	10	11	12	13	14	15
16	(17)	18	19	20	21	**22**
23	24	25	26	27	28	29
30						

October

M	T	W	T	F	S	S
	1	⬤2	3	4	5	6
7	8	9	10	11	12	13
14	15	16	(17)	18	19	20
21	22	23	24	25	26	27
28	29	30	**31**			

⬤ New Moons   ◯ Full Moons   ☐ Sabbats

March

M	T	W	T	F	S	S
				1	2	3
4	5	6	7	8	9	**10**
11	12	13	14	15	16	17
18	**19**	20	21	22	23	24
(25)	26	27	28	29	30	31

April

M	T	W	T	F	S	S
1	2	3	4	5	6	7
8	9	10	11	12	13	14
15	16	17	18	19	20	21
22	(23)	24	25	26	27	28
29	**30**					

July

M	T	W	T	F	S	S
1	2	3	4	**5**	6	7
8	9	10	11	12	13	14
15	16	17	18	19	20	(21)
22	23	24	25	26	27	28
29	30	31				

August

M	T	W	T	F	S	S
			1	**2**	3	**4**
5	6	7	8	9	10	11
12	13	14	15	16	17	18
(19)	20	21	22	23	24	25
26	27	28	29	30	31	

November

M	T	W	T	F	S	S
			1	2	3	
4	5	6	7	8	9	10
11	12	13	14	(15)	16	17
18	19	20	21	22	23	24
25	26	27	28	29	30	

December

M	T	W	T	F	S	S
						1
2	3	4	5	6	7	8
9	10	11	12	13	14	(15)
16	17	18	19	20	**21**	22
23	24	25	26	27	28	29
30	31					

It's a leap year! Every four years, we add an extra day to our calendars (February 29th).

Table of Contents

Key to Symbols

Events

✸	Sabbat
⊗	Exact Astronomical Cross-Quarter
●	New Moon
◐	First Quarter
○	Full Moon
◑	Third or Last Quarter

✪

Days marked with this symbol are likely to be lucky and highly magical. This is the witch's equivalent to what old almanacs term "good fishing days."

Zodiac Signs

♈	Aries
♉	Taurus
♊	Gemini
♋	Cancer
♌	Leo
♍	Virgo
♎	Libra
♏	Scorpio
♐	Sagittarius
♑	Capricorn
♒	Aquarius
♓	Pisces

Celestial Symbols

☽	Moon
☽v/c	Moon Void of Course
☼	Sun
⟡	Meteor Shower Peak
☿℞	Mercury Retrograde

The Moon appears next to its zodiac sign along with the time it enters that sign. For example, ☽♍ 1:18 am indicates that the Moon enters Virgo at 1:18 am Central Time.

The Moon is void of course when it is not forming any major aspects with other planets before entering into a new sign. The time at which this occurs is noted after the symbols such as, ☽v/c 8:59 pm indicating that the Moon is void of course at 8:59 pm Central Time. Void of course ends when the Moon enters the next zodiac sign.

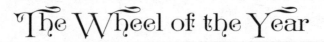

The Wheel of the Year

Sabbats are seasonal festivals known for their magical energy, celestial symmetry, and spiritual significance. Each Sabbat is known by various names, reflecting differences in traditions and teachings. One witch may refer to the June solstice as *Litha,* while another will call it *Midsummer.* Regardless of the names, most witches celebrate the eight classic Sabbats of four Quarters and four Cross-Quarters.

Establishing personal Sabbat traditions will help you grow and attune to the rhythms of the seasons. Your traditions create comforting anchors for your mind and spirit. You might prepare a special recipe every Yule, harvest magical herbs every Midsummer, or make candles every Imbolc. Explore the seasonal activities you enjoy, and incorporate them into your tradition.

Quarters

The four Quarter Sabbats are the two solstices and two equinoxes. These astrological events do not occur on the same day every year. The Quarter Sabbats divide the earth's path around the sun (the ecliptic) into quarters, falling 90° apart on the ecliptic.

Cross-Quarters

The four Cross-Quarters are traditional Sabbats that are celebrated at the same time every year. Their dates do not fall exactly halfway between the Quarter Sabbats. They include Imbolc (February 1-2), Beltane (April 30-May 1), Lughnasadh or Lammas (August 1-2), and Samhain (October 31-November 1).

Exact Astronomical Cross-Quarters

The exact astronomical Cross-Quarter Sabbats occur when the earth is precisely halfway along the ecliptic between a solstice and an equinox. The Quarters and astronomical Cross Quarters are 45° apart on the ecliptic. Pages 12-13 show the exact times and dates of each astronomical Cross-Quarter.

Many witches combine the traditional Cross-Quarter Sabbat dates with the astronomical Cross-Quarters. For example, traditional Samhain celebrations begin on October 31st and continue through November 1st. The astronomical Cross-Quarter date for Samhain is November 6th, and some witches celebrate Samhain from October 31st through November 6th.

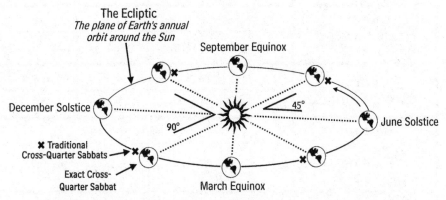

Traditional Cross-Quarter Sabbats are shown with ✖ and are just before the astronomical Cross-Quarters.

Northern & Southern Hemispheres

The Sabbat you celebrate on a particular date depends on your tradition and location. Witches in the Southern Hemisphere (SH) often learn their craft from materials written for the Northern Hemisphere (NH). These SH witches may observe the same Sabbats simultaneously as witches in the NH. However, SH witches sometimes choose to celebrate according to the local seasons. Rather than celebrate Beltane on May 1st, when it is autumn in the Southern Hemisphere, these witches may reverse the Sabbats and observe Samhain. Then on October 31st, they celebrate Beltane.

Remember, you are the authority in your practice!
You have the final say in which Sabbats you observe,
when you celebrate, and what names you use for them.

Sabbat Times & Dates

Northern Hemisphere

Sabbat	Eastern	Central	Pacific	GMT
Imbolc Candlemas Traditional Feb. 1-2	**February 4**			
	3:16 am	2:16 am	12:16 am	08:16 am
Ostara Spring Equinox	**March 19**			**March 20**
	11:06 am	*10:06 pm*	*8:06 am*	3:06 am
Beltane May Eve Traditional Apr. 30-May 1	**May 4**			
	7:59 pm	*6:59 pm*	*4:59 pm*	11:59 pm
Midsummer Litha Summer Solstice	**June 20**			
	4:50 pm	*3:50 pm*	*1:50 pm*	8:50 pm
Lughnasadh Lammas Traditional Aug. 1-2	**August 6**			**August 7**
	8:00 pm	*7:00 pm*	*5:00 pm*	12:00 am
Mabon Autumn Equinox	**September 22**			
	8:43 am	*7:43 am*	*5:43 am*	12:43 pm
Samhain Hallows Traditional Oct. 31-Nov. 1	**November 6**			
	5:10 pm	4:10 pm	2:10 pm	10:10 pm
Yule Winter Solstice	**December 21**			
	4:20 am	3:20 am	1:20 am	9:20 am

Time shown in *italics* is calculated for DST from Mar. 10th through Nov. 3rd.

Sabbat Times & Dates

Southern Hemisphere

Sabbat	GMT	Australia AEST	New Zealand NZST
Lughnasadh Lammas Traditional Aug. 1-2	**February 4**		
	08:16 am	6:16 pm	8:16 pm
Mabon Autumn Equinox	**March 20**		
	3:06 am	1:06 pm	3:06 pm
Samhain Hallows Traditional Oct. 31-Nov. 1	**May 4**	**May 5**	
	11:59 pm	9:59 am	11:59 am
Yule Winter Solstice	**June 20**	**June 21**	
	8:50 pm	6:50 am	8:50 am
Imbolc Candlemas Traditional Feb. 1-2	**August 7**		
	12:00 am	10:00 am	12:00 pm
Ostara Spring Equinox	**September 22**		**Sept. 23**
	12:43 pm	10:43 pm	12:43 am
Beltane May Eve Traditional Apr. 30-May 1	**November 6**	**November 7**	
	10:10 pm	8:10 am	10:10 am
Midsummer Litha Summer Solstice	**December 21**		
	9:20 am	7:20 pm	9:20 pm

Dec 30
4:26 pm
♑

Jan 11
5:57 am
♑

Feb 9
4:59 pm
♒

Dec 1
12:21 am
♐

Mar 10
4:00 am
♓

Nov 1
7:47 am
♏

Apr 8
1:20 pm
♈

Oct 2
1:49 pm
♎

May 7
10:21 pm
♉

Sep 2
8:55 pm
♍

Jun 6
7:37 am
♊

Aug 4
6:13 am
♌

Jul 5
5:57 pm
♋

THE NEW MOONS OF 2024

Notable New Moon Events

★ **Super New Moon:** Feb. 9, Mar. 10, Apr. 8

★ **Micro New Moon:** Oct. 2   ★ **Black Moon:** Dec. 30

THE FULL MOONS OF 2024

Jan 25
11:54 am
♌

Feb 24
6:30 am
♍

Mar 25
2:00 am
♎

Apr 23
6:48 pm
♏

May 23
8:53 am
♐

Jun 21
8:07 pm
♑

Jul 21
5:17 am
♑

Aug 19
1:25 pm
♒

Sep 17
9:34 pm
♓

Oct 17
6:26 am
♈

Nov 15
3:28 pm
♉

Dec 15
3:01 am
♊

Notable Full Moon Events

★ Supermoon: Sep. 17, Oct. 17 ★ Micro Moon: Feb. 24, Mar. 25

★ Blue Moon: Aug. 19 ★ Eclipse: Mar. 25 (penumbral), Sep. 17 (partial)

15

January

Mon	Tue	Wed	Thr	Fri	Sat	Sun
1 ☿R Ends	2	3 ◐	4	5	6	7
8	9	10	11 ●	12	13	14
15	16	17 ◐	18	19	20	21
22	23	24	25 ○	26	27	28
29	30	31				

• National Blood Donor Month
• National Braille Literacy Month
• National Hobby Month
• National Hot Tea Month

Notes

_____
_____
_____
_____
_____

1	◑
2	◑
3	◑
4	◑
5	◑
6	◑
7	◑
8	◑
9	●
10	●
11	●
12	●
13	●
14	●
15	◐
16	◐
17	◐
18	◐
19	◐
20	◐
21	○
22	◐
23	○
24	○
25	○
26	○
27	○
28	○
29	○
30	◑
31	◑

Hecate & Trivia

Trivia is a Roman Goddess equated with the Greek Goddess Hecate[1]. She has power over crossroads, graveyards, transitions, and liminal spaces. Like Hecate, she is a triple-form deity and her domain is sorcery and witchcraft.

Transitioning into a new year is the perfect time for a ritual for Hecate and Trivia. Adapt this ritual to align with your personal beliefs and practices while honoring the ancient traditions associated with Hecate and Trivia.

Materials:

A black cloth | three black candles | a small bowl of earth or salt | a key or a symbolic object representing a crossroads | incense or herb bundle (preferably mugwort, myrrh, or patchouli) | a small offering such as herbs, flowers, or a heartfelt written note.

Procedure:

Find a secluded outdoor location with a crossroads or create a crossroads symbol using stones or chalk. Lay the black cloth at the center of the crossroads to serve as your altar. Light the three black candles, placing them in a triangle formation around the altar. Sprinkle a pinch of earth or salt on the altar to symbolize grounding and connection. Light the incense and let the smoke rise, representing the bridge between realms. Hold the key or symbolic object and speak your intentions, inviting Hecate to join you and guide your path. Place your offering on the altar, expressing gratitude and respect. Close your eyes, breathe deeply, and visualize a luminous crossroads connecting you with Hecate's presence. Meditate, listen, and be receptive to any messages or insights that come to you. You may feel your connection to the Goddess immediately or notice it strengthen over the next few months. When you feel ready, thank Hecate for her presence and guidance. Safely extinguish the candles and incense, leaving the crossroads as you found it.

Trivia: Although we celebrate the equinox as the time when day and night are of equal length, the actual time this occurs is known as equilux. The exact date of the equilux depends on your location, but it is always before the spring equinox and after the autumn equinox.

Monday 1

☿℞ Ends
☽♍ since 5:54 am December 31, 2023
New Year's Day (U.S. Federal Holiday)

Tuesday 2

☽v/c 4:12 pm - ☽♎ 6:47 pm

Wednesday 3

◑ 9:30 pm
Festival of Sleep Day
☄ Quadrantids Meteor Shower

Thursday 4

Trivia Day
☽v/c 4:24 pm
☄ Quadrantids Meteor Shower

Friday 5

☽♏ 6:40 am
Befana Day

Saturday 6

☽v/c 1:12 pm

Sunday 7

☽ ♐ 3:09 pm

Magical Teas & Tisanes

Making your own tea and tisane[2] blends is very rewarding! Stock your apothecary with these core herbs to make magical brews quick and easy. Experiment with making teas from these herbs, using the recipes in the back of your almanac as a guide. Brew your tea using one rounded teaspoon of your blend per cup, steep for 3-5 minutes, and enjoy.

★ **Tea** *Camellia sinensis* — Black, green, or semi-fermented like Darjeeling and oolong. Taste your tea brewed alone to experience each tea's nuanced flavors before blending.

★ **Hibiscus** *Hibiscus sabdariffa* — Hibiscus flowers make a deep red, tangy liquor high in antioxidants. Used for passion, manifestation, psychic and dream work, and vitality.

★ **Peppermint** *Mentha x piperita* — Peppermint's great minty flavor and fragrance blends well with green tea. Used for prosperity, purification, divination, and attraction.

★ **Rose Hips** *Rosa canina and Rosa rubiginosa* — Pieces are easier to use than whole rose hips. Very high in vitamin C and antioxidants. Tangy liquor blends well with hibiscus. Used for love, vitality, protection, beauty, and connecting with nature.

★ **Elderberries** *Sambucus nigra* — Dried berries impart a light fruity flavor and antioxidants. Used for protection, warding, magical and psychic power, vitality.

★ **Chamomile** *Matricaria chamomilla* — Imparts a honey-apple aroma and a golden color to your brews. Relaxing and soothing, it is used for purification, dreams, peace, meditation, luck, visions, and protection.

★ **Lemon Verbena** *Aloysia citriodora* — Superior lemon scent and flavor. Used for attraction, purification, banishing, nightmare prevention, and breaking bonds.

★ **Cinnamon** *Cinnamomum verum* — Bark chips are easy to use and impart a sweet, spicy flavor. Used for attraction, blessings, purification, protection, and magic.

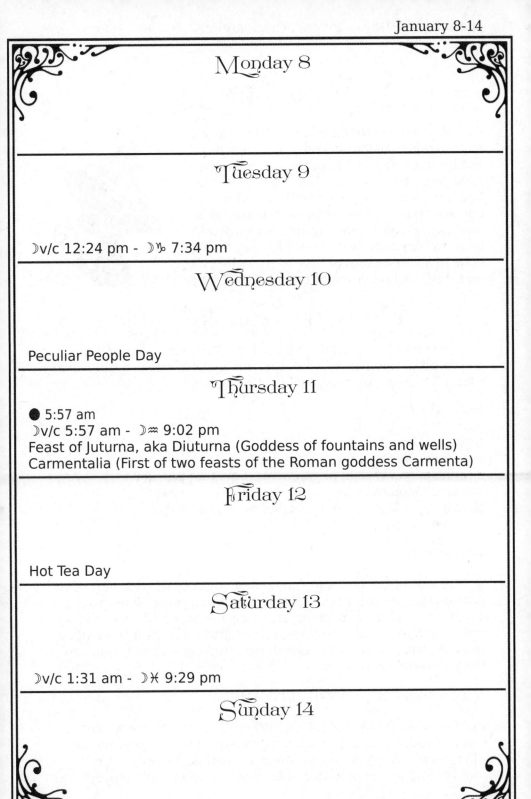

Monday 8

Tuesday 9

☽v/c 12:24 pm - ☽♑ 7:34 pm

Wednesday 10

Peculiar People Day

Thursday 11

● 5:57 am
☽v/c 5:57 am - ☽♒ 9:02 pm
Feast of Juturna, aka Diuturna (Goddess of fountains and wells)
Carmentalia (First of two feasts of the Roman goddess Carmenta)

Friday 12

Hot Tea Day

Saturday 13

☽v/c 1:31 am - ☽♓ 9:29 pm

Sunday 14

National Hat Day
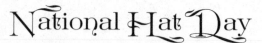

Every day is a good day to celebrate, and National Hat Day gives us a lighthearted theme to explore. This occasion invites you to express your personality. Beyond being a fashion accessory, hats symbolize identity, culture, and even occupation, making this day an excellent opportunity to appreciate hats' rich history and versatility. So, dust off your favorite headgear, put it on with pride, and join the festivities of National Hat Day.

Protein Granola Balls

These quick, no-bake treats are packed with energy. They can be stored in an airtight container for up to a week in the refrigerator, or over three months in the freezer.

Ingredients

1 cup instant oats
½ cup creamy peanut butter
2 tablespoons vanilla or unflavored protein powder
½ cup chocolate chips
¼ cup dried fruit such as raisins or cranberries
⅓ cup coconut flakes

Directions

Mix half of the coconut flakes in a small bowl with half of the protein powder. Combine all the remaining ingredients in a separate bowl. Knead the mixture until it is mixed well. Refrigerate for half an hour and then form into balls. Roll the balls in the coconut flake/protein powder mixture and return them to the refrigerator to set up.

Variation for Sabbat Treats

Instead of forming the dough into balls, press it into a silicone candy mold. Crescent moon shapes work well for this recipe. Freeze the filled molds for an hour. Pop the dough out of the molds and sprinkle with the coconut flake/protein powder mix.

Monday 15

National Hat Day
☽v/c 2:46 pm - ☽♈ 10:49 pm
Martin Luther King Jr. Day (U.S. Federal Holiday)
Carmentalia (Second of two feasts of Carmenta)

Tuesday 16

Appreciate a Dragon Day

Wednesday 17

☽ 9:52 am
☽v/c 9:52 pm

Thursday 18

☽♉ 2:12 am

Friday 19

Saturday 20

☀♒ 8:08 am
☽v/c 7:56 am - ☽♊ 7:58 am

Sunday 21

World Religion Day
National Granola Bar Day

Dice Divination

Dice divination has existed for thousands of years, and the technique has many different approaches. The list of meanings below is one approach using three ordinary game dice, or one D18 (eighteen-sided) die. If you are proficient in numerology, your interpretations will differ from those provided for dice. You can interpret your roll based on numerology alone or combine it with these meanings.

Draw a circle about eight inches across and toss your dice. Interpret the dice that land inside the circle, ignoring those that fall outside of the circle.

Dice Roll Meanings

1. Family quarrels, standing alone, a bad omen.
2. Partnerships, assess situations carefully.
3. Social life, pleasant surprise, sudden change.
4. Misunderstandings, setbacks, order.
5. Change, plans progressing, unexpected info or help.
6. Misfortune, possible loss, family situations.
7. Challenges, financial difficulties, gossip.
8. Success, proceed with caution, prosperity.
9. Reconciliation, love, endings and beginnings.
10. Success, honor, promotion, news, birth and rebirth.
11. Spiritual growth and enlightenment, separation.
12. Life-changing advice and messages, seek counsel.
13. Transformation, magic around, grief.
14. Danger, help from others.
15. Deception around, occult energies, caution needed.
16. Enjoyable trips and travel.
17. Change perspective, sound advice from strangers.
18. Good fortune, success, achieving goals.

Tarot Adaptation

If you are already familiar with the meanings of the major arcana tarot cards, you can use a D22 die (twenty-two-sided) along with your current knowledge of the tarot. It is difficult to find dice that begin with a zero, so for this method, a roll of 22 represents the Fool card, while all other numbers directly correspond to the numbers of the major arcana.

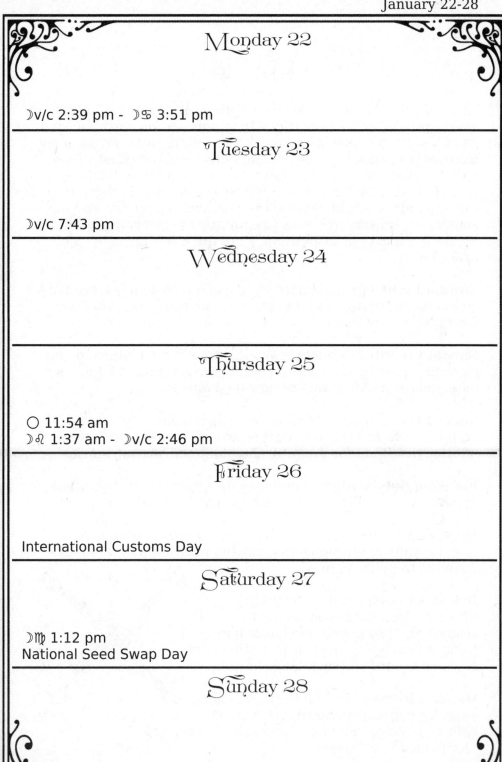

Monday 22

☽v/c 2:39 pm - ☽♋ 3:51 pm

Tuesday 23

☽v/c 7:43 pm

Wednesday 24

Thursday 25

○ 11:54 am
☽♌ 1:37 am - ☽v/c 2:46 pm

Friday 26

International Customs Day

Saturday 27

☽♍ 1:12 pm
National Seed Swap Day

Sunday 28

Imbolc

Imbolc is a time of renewal and preparation for the coming year's growth. Witches participate in purification and cleansing rituals while considering goals for the coming year. Physical and magical housekeeping are popular activities. The exact Cross Quarter event occurs a few days after the traditional Sabbat date. Imbolc, also known as Brigid's Day, is named after the Celtic goddess Brigid, associated with healing, poetry, and smithcraft. Imbolc invites us to embrace the returning light and kindle the sparks of inspiration. Here are a few ideas to celebrate Imbolc:

Candle Lighting: Illuminate your space with candles, symbolizing the sun's return. Light them in each room, invoking the warmth and energy of the growing light.

Spring Cleaning: Imbolc is an ideal time for decluttering and cleansing your living environment. Clear out physical and energetic debris, making way for new beginnings.

Sacred Fires: If permitted, have a small bonfire outdoors or light a hearth fire indoors. Gather around it with loved ones, offering gratitude for the returning light and sharing stories.

Planting Seeds: Start planning your garden for the upcoming growing season. Plant seeds or bless seeds for later planting.

Poetry and Music: Imbolc celebrates creativity and inspiration. Engage in writing poetry, playing musical instruments, or listening to uplifting music.

Brigid's Cross: Craft a traditional Brigid's Cross from reeds or straw, symbolizing protection and blessings. Hang it above your door or in a prominent place as a ward and luck talisman.

Healing Rituals: Invoke Brigid's healing energies by performing rituals such as energy healing, Reiki, or creating herbal remedies for personal well-being.

Monday 29

☽v/c 5:37 am

Tuesday 30

☽♎ 2:04 am

Wednesday 31

Hecate Night

Thursday 1

❁ Imbolc Eve
☽v/c 3:02 am - ☽♏ 2:37 pm

Friday 2

❁ Imbolc
◑ 5:18 pm
Groundhog Day
World Wetlands Day

Saturday 3

☽v/c 9:24 pm

Sunday 4

⊗ 2:16 am
☽♐ 12:28 am
Rosa Parks Day
World Cancer Day

February

Mon	Tue	Wed	Thr	Fri	Sat	Sun
			1 ✿	2 ✿ ◐	3	4 ⊗
5	6	7	8	9 ●	10	11
12	13	14	15	16 ◐	17	18
19	20	21	22	23	24 ○	25
26	27	28	29			

- Black History Month (U.S.)
- LGBTQIA+ History Month (UK)
- Great American Pie Month

Notes

_____

_____

_____

_____

_____

1	◖	
2	◑	
3	◑	
4	◑	
5	◑	
6	●	
7	●	
8	●	
9	●	
10	●	
11	●	
12	◐	
13	◐	
14	◐	
15	◐	
16	◐	
17	◐	
18	◐	
19	◐	
20	◐	
21	○	
22	○	
23	○	
24	○	
25	○	
26	○	
27	○	
28	◗	
29	◗	

Year of the Wood Dragon

Chinese New Year is the official name of this week's holiday, but its more inclusive name is the Lunar New Year. Celebrated by many East Asian cultures and worldwide, this year is the year of the wood dragon. The dragon is one of the twelve Chinese zodiac signs. It represents power, success, luck, and nobility. The wood dragon is known for its curiosity and diplomacy, promising this to be an auspicious year.

Tarot Biases

Two major arcana tarot cards represent what our culture deems "feminine power." However, many books from the 20th century reflect sexual biases in their interpretations of these cards.

The High Priestess holds secrets and mysteries, yet many books from the last century indicate that this card represents lies and infidelity. Similarly, The Moon can represent an uncertain path you must tread intuitively, while classic keywords for this card often include deception and sabotage.

Although these 20th century associations may apply to a specific reading, consider the biases that influenced their common meanings in the past.

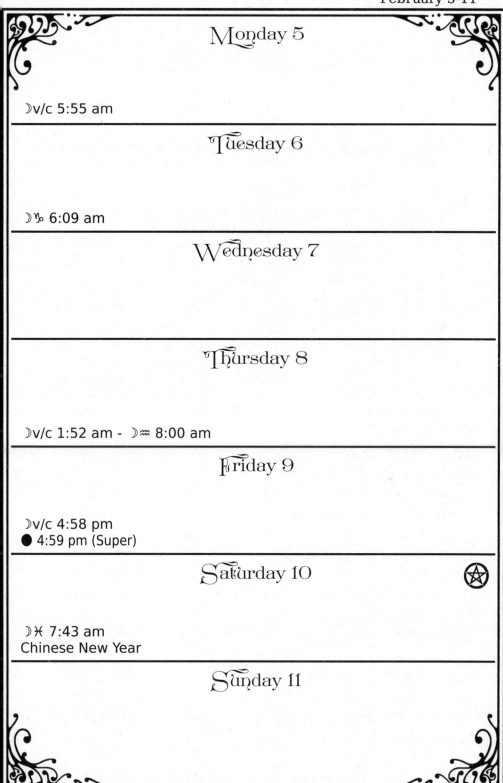

Monday 5

☽v/c 5:55 am

Tuesday 6

☽♑ 6:09 am

Wednesday 7

Thursday 8

☽v/c 1:52 am - ☽♒ 8:00 am

Friday 9

☽v/c 4:58 pm
● 4:59 pm (Super)

Saturday 10

☽♓ 7:43 am
Chinese New Year

Sunday 11

Essential Oils for Candles & Incense

It takes fifteen pounds of lavender flowers to yield an ounce of essential oil. A single drop of essential oil has intense energy, but when making candles and incense, you may need more oils for their fragrance.

Container candles use up to 9% essential oils, requiring almost an ounce to make a ten-ounce candle. Because candles and incense are ignited, you must consider the flashpoint[3] of your selected oils. Rosemary essential oil has a flashpoint of around 112°F/44°C. If you use an ounce of oil in a ten-ounce candle, the entire wax surface may erupt in flame. To avoid this, choose essential oils with a flashpoint over 170°F/77°C. If you use oils with lower flashpoints, do so <u>very</u> sparingly. A drop of rosemary essential oil in a ten-ounce candle will boost its purification and protection properties without causing flare-up issues.

The following is a list of my favorite essential oils with high flashpoints for candles, incense, and other flammable crafts. Oils below the 170°F/77°C threshold should only be used in quantities up to 5% in candles.

Atlas Cedar (*Cedrus atlantica*)	220°F (104°C)
Basil (*Ocimum Basilicum*)	165°F (74°C)
Cinnamon Bark (*Cinnamomum verum*)	190°F (88°C)
Cinnamon Leaf (*Cinnamomum cassia*)	190°F (88°C)
Citronella (*Cymbopogon Winterianus Jowitt*)	167°F (75°C)
Clary Sage (*Salvia Sclarea*)	169°F (76°C)
Clove Bud (*Eugenia caryophyllus*)	205°F (96°C)
Geranium (*Pelargonium graveolens*)	176°F (80°C)
Myrrh (*Commiphora myrrha*)	212°F (100°C)
Neroli (*Citrus aurantium*)	167°F (75°C)
Palmarosa (*Cymbopogon martinii*)	203°F (95°C)
Patchouli (*Pogostemon cablin*)	230°F (110°C)
Sandalwood (*Santalum album*)	200°F (93°C)
Vetivert (*Vetivera zizanioides*)	230°F (110°C)
Ylang Ylang (*Cananga odorata*)	212°F (100°C)

Monday 12

☽v/c 6:32 am ☽♈ 7:26 am

Tuesday 13

⛤

Mardi Gras

Wednesday 14

Valentine's Day
☽v/c 4:20 am - ☽♉ 9:30 am

Thursday 15

Lupercalia

Friday 16

☽ 11:10 pm
☽v/c 9:00 am - ☽♊ 1:40 pm

Saturday 17

Sunday 18

✳♓ 10:13 pm
☽v/c 9:20 pm - ☽♋ 9:25 pm

Pop Culture Witchcraft

The past twenty-five years have brought us a powerful resurgence of witchcraft in popular culture. Movies like *The Craft* and television series like *Charmed* and *Buffy the Vampire Slayer* helped drive interest in the non-fiction aspects of magic and witchcraft. The Harry Potter book series enchanted multiple generations and increased interest in real-life witchcraft.

Those who were already practitioners during this period were both enraged and delighted. The outrageous inaccuracies of pop culture's portrayal of our spiritual traditions left us feeling deflated. We'd already spent much of our lives trying to set the record straight about Wicca, witchcraft, and Paganism. Our efforts towards anti-defamation seemed so minuscule when huge, well-funded studios could produce so much misinformation so quickly. And yet — many of us felt a bit of delight. These were good stories! The child in all of us reveled in the exciting adventures and beautiful sets, costumes, and special effects. We learned that pop culture inspires people to ask questions about real witchcraft.

Many fictional portrayals use information from real witchcraft, occultism, and folk traditions. Jim Butcher's book series *The Dresden Files* features concepts of sympathetic magic used in all magical practices. In *Buffy the Vampire Slayer*, the character Willow explores her budding powers like the sisters in the series *Charmed*. Many of us could relate to the anxiety and excitement of realizing we have interests and talents in areas our society deems either fantasy or evil.

The enchanting world of witches in pop culture continues to weave its spell over the entertainment industry, leaving an indelible mark on the collective imagination. While some portrayals of witchcraft are deeply offensive, it is vital to understand how pop culture portrays our traditions and influences public attitudes.

Think about how pop culture has impacted your path. What films, music, books, or series have you enjoyed? Which ones disappointed you, and which made you ask more questions? In next week's article, we'll delve into specific pop culture references to witchcraft, exploring its portrayal across various mediums.

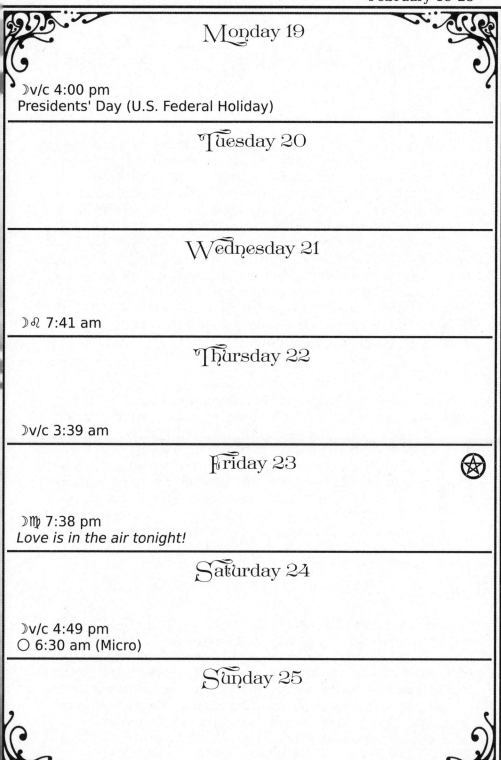

Monday 19

☽v/c 4:00 pm
Presidents' Day (U.S. Federal Holiday)

Tuesday 20

Wednesday 21

☽♌ 7:41 am

Thursday 22

☽v/c 3:39 am

Friday 23

☽♍ 7:38 pm
Love is in the air tonight!

Saturday 24

☽v/c 4:49 pm
○ 6:30 am (Micro)

Sunday 25

Witchy Television, Film & Music

Television

Television invites viewers into mesmerizing realms of magic and intrigue. Shows like *Chilling Adventures of Sabrina* and *American Horror Story: Coven* portray contemporary witches, blending elements of horror, fantasy, and occultism. These series spark conversations about feminism, empowerment, and the exploration of spirituality through witchcraft. *The Witcher* fantasy series includes characters with magical abilities. *Legacies* is a spin-off of *The Vampire Diaries* and *The Originals*. The series incorporates witchcraft and supernatural elements. Set in an alternate present, *Motherland: Fort Salem* explores a world where witches ended their persecution 300 years ago by allying with the U.S. government. It follows a group of young witches training to become combat units.

Movies & Film

In cinema, films like *The Witch*, *Suspiria*, and *The Craft: Legacy* have revived the fascination with witchcraft, offering nuanced portrayals that delve into the complexity of witch characters and their relationships with power, identity, and the supernatural. *The Witches* follows a young boy who uncovers a coven of witches planning to turn children into mice, reflecting the persistent attitude that witches hurt children. *Coven of Sisters* is a historical drama about a group of young women accused of witchcraft during the Spanish Inquisition. This November, *Wicked: Part One* (a film adaptation of the stage musical) will be released.

Music

Musicians like Florence + The Machine, Lana Del Rey, and Hozier have evoked the ethereal allure of witches, infusing their songs with haunting melodies, occult symbolism, and references to magical rituals. "Witch Hunt" is a folk-infused track by the band Haim that addresses themes of persecution and injustice, drawing parallels to historical witch hunts. "Coven" by High Priestess pays homage to witchcraft, combining heavy, doom-laden riffs with ethereal vocals.

Monday 26

☽♎ 8:30 am

Tuesday 27

☽v/c 12:21 pm

Wednesday 28

☽♏ 9:09 pm

Thursday 29

Leap Day

Friday 1

☽v/c 7:08 am

Saturday 2

☽♐ 7:56 am

Sunday 3

◐ 9:23 am
☽v/c 10:00 pm

March

Mon	Tue	Wed	Thr	Fri	Sat	Sun
				1	2	3 ◑
4	5	6	7	8	9	10 ●
11	12	13	14	15	16 ◐	17
18	19 ✸	20	21	22	23	24
25 ○	26	27	28	29	30	31

- National Women's History Month
- National Craft Month
- National Nutrition Month

Notes

_____

_____

_____

_____

_____

1	◑	
2	◑	
3	◑	
4	◑	
5	◑	
6	◑	
7	◑	
8	◑	
9	●	
10	●	
11	●	
12	●	
13	◐	
14	◐	
15	◐	
16	◐	
17	◐	
18	◐	
19	◐	
20	◐	
21	○	
22	○	
23	○	
24	○	
25	○	
26	○	
27	○	
28	◑	
29	◑	
30	◑	
31	◑	

Grounding Ritual

Grounding rituals like this can be rejuvenating and help deepen your connection with the healing energy of nature. Earth energy is potent, so approach this ritual with respect and reverence. Feel free to incorporate some personal touches to make it a meaningful experience.

- Find a quiet and comfortable space. Choose an outdoor location such as a garden or park, but indoors works just as well.
- Stand barefoot on the ground or sit with your palms resting on the earth or the floor. Take a few deep breaths, close your eyes, and imagine roots growing from the soles of your feet, anchoring you to the earth. If you are indoors, visualize the roots going through the layers of the building and into the ground.
- Imagine drawing up energy from the earth, feeling its stability and grounding power.
- Repeat affirmations or silently express gratitude for the earth's support.
- Take a few more deep breaths, allowing the earth's energy to fill your body.
- When you feel ready, slowly release the visualization and thank the earth for its grounding energy.

Holding a moss agate, jasper, obsidian, or other grounding stone may help you connect to the earth's energy. Stones can be beneficial when you are performing grounding rituals indoors.

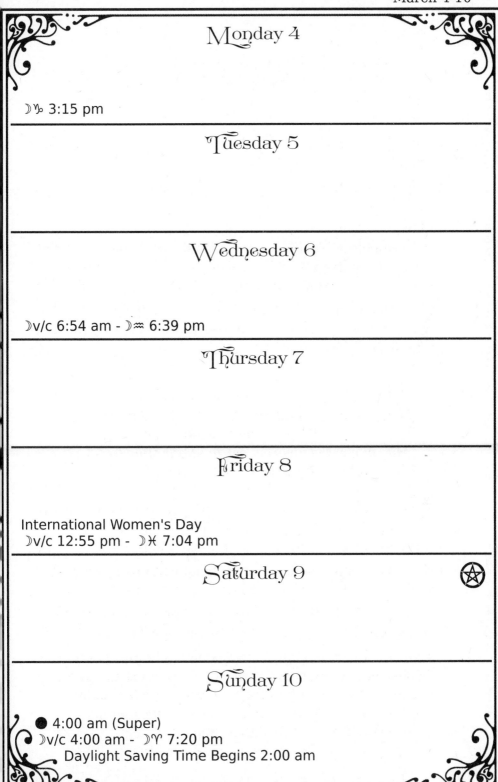

Monday 4

☽♑ 3:15 pm

Tuesday 5

Wednesday 6

☽v/c 6:54 am - ☽♒ 6:39 pm

Thursday 7

Friday 8

International Women's Day
☽v/c 12:55 pm - ☽♓ 7:04 pm

Saturday 9

Sunday 10

● 4:00 am (Super)
☽v/c 4:00 am - ☽♈ 7:20 pm
Daylight Saving Time Begins 2:00 am

Bond Breaking Ritual

Ingredients

- Black Obsidian
- Mugwort
- Black Candle

Directions

- Hold the black obsidian in your hand, close your eyes, and take several deep breaths. Visualize a strong, protective barrier around you, shielding you from unwanted energies.

- Light the black candle and place it on a safe surface. As it burns, focus on the flame and repeat the following incantation three times:

With this flame, I sever the ties that bind.
Let the connection between [name] and [name]
dissolve and unwind.
May our paths diverge, setting both of us free.
By my will, so mote it be.

- Take a pinch of mugwort and sprinkle it around the candle, forming a circle. Envision the herb's energy cutting through any energetic cords or connections.

- Hold the black obsidian in your hand and imagine a dark void expanding between you and the other person.

- Place the black obsidian near the candle, visualizing it acting as a barrier, preventing further connections.

- Allow the candle to burn down completely, and safely dispose of any remnants of the spell except the obsidian. Keep the stone near you for a month to prevent bonds from reforming. After a month, the obsidian can be cleansed and re-used for other magic.

Monday 11

Tuesday 12

☽v/c 6:07 am - ☽♉ 7:29 pm

Wednesday 13

Thursday 14

Pi Day
☽v/c 12:56 am - ☽♊ 10:16 pm

Friday 15

Saturday 16

☽ 11:10 pm
☽v/c 11:10 pm

Sunday 17

☽♋ 4:41 am
St. Patrick's Day

Ostara

Ostara heralds the arrival of spring and celebrates the balance between light and dark. It is an excellent time to magically and physically set the foundations of a project and is a time of fertility, rebirth, and the awakening of nature. Here are a few ideas to embrace the spirit of Ostara:

Egg Decorating: Eggs symbolize the fertility and renewal of nature. Decorate eggs with vibrant colors, symbols, sigils, and patterns representing your goals. Use them as altar decorations for the season, hang them in your home as talismans to help you attain your goals, or use them in an egg hunt.

Planting Ritual: Prepare your garden for the growing season by planting seeds or transplants. Focus your intention on growth and nurturing yourself and the earth.

Nature Walk: Take a mindful walk in nature, observing the signs of spring's arrival. Appreciate the blossoming flowers, migratory birds' return, and the natural world's awakening.

Spring Cleaning: Embrace the tradition of spring cleaning, not only in your physical space but also in your energetic and spiritual realms. Smoke cleanse or use your besom to help clear out stagnant energy and make way for fresh beginnings.

Floral Offerings: Create an altar adorned with flowers, representing the beauty and vitality of the season. Offer them as gifts to the earth or as offerings to deities associated with spring.

Ostara Feast: Prepare a feast featuring seasonal fresh fruits, vegetables, and light dishes. Incorporate traditional symbols such as eggs, honey, and sprouts to honor the fertility and abundance of the season.

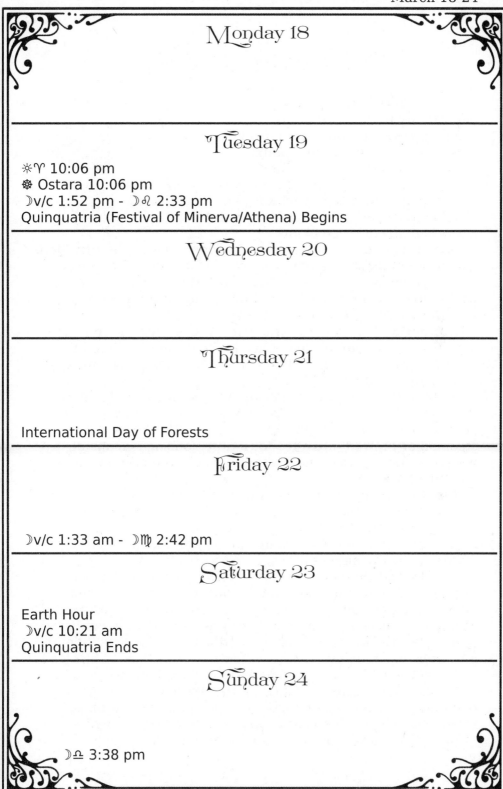

Monday 18

Tuesday 19

☀♈ 10:06 pm
❀ Ostara 10:06 pm
☽v/c 1:52 pm - ☽♌ 2:33 pm
Quinquatria (Festival of Minerva/Athena) Begins

Wednesday 20

Thursday 21

International Day of Forests

Friday 22

☽v/c 1:33 am - ☽♍ 2:42 pm

Saturday 23

Earth Hour
☽v/c 10:21 am
Quinquatria Ends

Sunday 24

☽♎ 3:38 pm

Wildcrafting Weeds

Weed Appreciation Day is an opportunity to focus on some common weeds that are often over-looked. Many of these wild plants possess remarkable properties you can harness for various beneficial uses. Discovering the hidden potential within common weeds enables us to develop a deeper connection with nature and access the many benefits of these plants.

It is crucial to research and learn about proper identification and sustainable harvesting practices before engaging in wild-crafting endeavors. Harvest only where it is legally allowed and where poisons or vehicle-related toxins are absent. Do your research before consuming any plants.

Dandelion (*Taraxacum officinale*) — The young leaves make a nutritious addition to salads, while the dried roots can be brewed into a soothing herbal tea. Dandelion is associated with love, wishes, balance, and joy.

Nettle (*Urtica dioica*) — Packed with vitamins and minerals, this plant offers nourishment and alleviates allergies, promotes healthy skin, and supports joint health. Nettle leaves can be steamed or brewed into a tea for a nutritious and cleansing beverage. Use nettle in magic for healing, protection, vitality, and binding.

Plantain (*Plantago* spp.) — Plantain leaves can be used topi-cally to soothe insect bites, burns, and minor wounds. It is a gentle expectorant and can help ease coughs and respiratory congestion. Plantain offers magical and spiritual protection, wards against baneful entities, and boosts energy.

Chickweed (*Stellaria media*) — This humble weed is a trea-sure trove of nutrition, boasting high levels of vitamins and minerals. Chickweed can be incorporated into salads or cooked as a nutritious vegetable. It supports skin health and soothes minor skin irritations. Use chickweed in magic for love, fidelity, persistence, and beauty.

Purslane (*Portulaca oleracea*) — Purslane is rich in omega-3 fatty acids and antioxidants. Often regarded as a weed, this plant offers exceptional nutritional value and can be enjoyed fresh in salads or cooked as a side dish. Use magically to protect from hexes, psychic attacks, and nightmares.

Monday 25

○ 2:00 am (Micro)
Penumbral Lunar Eclipse

Tuesday 26

☽v/c 6:08 pm

Wednesday 27

☽♏ 4:03 am

Thursday 28

☽v/c 10:01 pm
National Weed Appreciation Day

Friday 29

☽♐ 2:52 pm

Saturday 30

Sunday 31

Easter Sunday
☽v/c 5:53 pm - ☽♑ 11:05 pm
International Transgender Day of Visibility

April

Mon	Tue	Wed	Thr	Fri	Sat	Sun
1 ☿R ◗	2	3	4	5	6	7
8 ●	9	10	11	12	13	14
15 ◖	16	17	18	19	20	21
22	23 ○	24	25 ☿R Ends	26	27	28
29	30 ✹					

- Child Abuse Prevention Month
- National Autism Awareness Month
- Sexual Assault Awareness Month
- National Garden Month

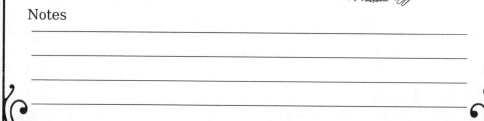

Notes

_____

_____

_____

_____

_____

1	◑	
2	◑	
3	◑	
4	◑	
5	◕	
6	◕	
7	●	
8	●	
9	●	
10	●	
11	◖	
12	◖	
13	◗	
14	◐	
15	◐	
16	◐	
17	◐	
18	◖	
19	○	
20	○	
21	○	
22	○	
23	○	
24	○	
25	○	
26	◗	
27	◗	
28	◗	
29	◑	
30	◑	

The Fool Tarot Card

Often depicted as a carefree wanderer on a journey, the Fool tarot card carries a profound message of embracing life's possibilities and stepping into the unknown with an open heart. While it may signify unpredictability or naivety, the Fool also represents a sense of fearlessness, spontaneity, and a willingness to take risks.

By embracing the positive aspects of the Fool, we can cultivate a sense of adventure, embrace new beginnings, trust our intuition, and welcome the opportunities that lie ahead. With an open mind and a light-hearted spirit, we can navigate life's twists and turns, embarking on transformative journeys that lead to personal growth and fulfillment.

The Fool's Journey Meditation

Find a quiet space where you can sit comfortably. Close your eyes and take a few deep breaths, allowing yourself to relax and release any tension. Visualize yourself as the carefree Fool, standing at the edge of a cliff, ready to embark on a new journey. Feel a sense of excitement and anticipation for what lies ahead. Embrace the feeling of fearlessness and trust in the unknown. If you wish, you may repeat this affirmation:

I embrace the positive aspects of the Fool.
I welcome new beginnings and trust in my intuition.

Take a few more deep breaths, feeling the energy of the Fool within you. When you're ready, slowly open your eyes and carry the spirit of the Fool with you throughout your day.

Monday 1

☿℞
☽ 10:14 pm
April Fool's Day
Veneralia (Feast of Venus/Aphrodite)

Tuesday 2

☽v/c 11:57 pm

Wednesday 3

☽♒ 4:08 am

Thursday 4

Friday 5

☽v/c 12:39 am - ☽♓ 6:13 am

Saturday 6

☽v/c 12:12 pm

Sunday 7

☽♈ 6:25 am

Choosing a Magical Name

Selecting a magical name is an empowering and deeply personal ritual that allows individuals to connect with their inner magic and embrace their spiritual identity. A name chosen for magical purposes holds immense significance, symbolically representing one's true essence and the energies one seeks to embody. When choosing a magical name, consider the following:

Intuition — Listen to your intuition and explore the names that resonate with your being. Trust the inner voice that guides you toward names that evoke a sense of power, enchantment, or alignment with your spiritual path.

Symbolism — Delve into the rich world of symbolism and explore the meanings behind names, elements, deities, or magical associations that hold personal significance to you. Choose a name that embodies qualities you wish to cultivate or expresses your magical intentions.

Ancestral Connections — Honor your ancestral heritage by incorporating family names or traditions into your magical name. This connection can deepen your sense of lineage and spiritual roots.

Creativity — Embrace your creative spirit and allow it to guide you in crafting a unique and enchanting name. Combine words, elements, or sounds that resonate with you and evoke a sense of mysticism.

Numerology — Some witches consider the numerological meaning of their names. Refer to the back of your almanac to calculate the numerological equivalent of names.

Ritual and Dedication — Engage in a ceremony to officially bestow your chosen name upon yourself. Your ritual can include meditation, setting intentions, lighting candles, or seeking the blessings of deities or spiritual guides. An invocation you can use in your ritual is on page 118. You may look into a mirror and repeat your chosen name or stand in a ritual circle declaring your name in a firm, confident voice.

Allow your chosen name to be a source of empowerment, reminding you of the infinite potential within and the magical connections you share with the world around you. Your chosen name is part of your journey that unfolds as you grow and evolve along your path. You may change your magical name over the years or add additional names to your magical identity.

Monday 8

☽v/c 9:38 pm
● 1:20 pm (Super)
International Romani Day

Tuesday 9

☽♉ 6:24 am
National Name Yourself Day
National *Library Workers* Day

Wednesday 10

☽v/c 2:19 pm

Thursday 11

☽♊ 7:59 am

Friday 12

Cerealia (Festival of Ceres/Demeter) Begins

Saturday 13

☽v/c 1:34 am - ☽♋ 12:45 pm

Sunday 14

Mushroom Magic

Mushrooms, with their enchanting forms and mysterious nature, have captivated our imaginations for centuries. Beyond their culinary uses, mushrooms have played significant roles in folklore, spirituality, and medicinal practices, showcasing a rich tapestry of magic and mystery throughout history. Mushrooms have influenced ancient civilizations, appeared in cave paintings, religious rituals, and mythical tales, representing the bridge between the earthly and the divine realms.

Throughout medieval Europe, mushrooms were associated with witchcraft and magical practices. Folklore intertwined mushrooms with fairy tales, envisioning them as portals to hidden realms or dwellings of mythical creatures. The allure and danger surrounding certain species contributed to their mystique.

Traditional healing systems, such as Chinese and Ayurvedic medicine, recognized the medicinal properties of mushrooms. These fungi are believed to possess powerful healing properties, offering remedies for various ailments and boosting vitality.

The discovery of psychoactive mushrooms, such as the *Psilocybe* genus, opened doors to altered states of consciousness, psychological healing, and spiritual exploration. Indigenous cultures incorporate these mushrooms into sacred ceremonies, enabling participants to experience visions, introspection, and expanded awareness.

In modern times, scientific research has unveiled the pharmacological potential of mushrooms, highlighting their ability to stimulate the immune system, combat inflammation, and even exhibit anti-cancer properties. This emerging field merges ancient wisdom with contemporary knowledge, shedding new light on the remarkable properties of mushrooms.

You can purchase fresh mushrooms at your local farmer's market or grocer and use them in rituals and spells. They are said to bridge the connection to the spiritual world and are associated with fertility, transformation, abundance, healing, and spiritual enlightenment.

Monday 15

Tax Day
☽ 2:13 pm
World Art Day
☽v/c 2:12 pm - ☽♌ 9:24 pm

Tuesday 16

Day of the Mushroom

Wednesday 17

Thursday 18

☽v/c 7:01 am - ☽♍ 9:11 am

Friday 19

Bicycle Day
☼♉ 9:00 am
Cerealia Ends

Saturday 20

☽v/c 6:09 am - ☽♎10:09 pm

Sunday 21

Festival Season Begins!

Beltane to Samhain is the busiest festival season for witches and Pagans. Festivals allow you to meet like-minded people, celebrate, worship, learn, and shop. Every festival has different vibes, amenities, and programs. There is usually live entertainment, such as music or fire dancing, and vendors provide food and unique products. Most festivals offer some space for camping. Posh events are sometimes held at hotels or retreats.

You can attend public rituals and presentations by "big-name-Pagans" such as authors or artists. You'll usually find a drum circle somewhere on the grounds, even when unscheduled. Large Pagan festivals are usually family-friendly. Nearly all are LGBTQIA+ friendly. Sexually explicit behavior is unwelcome at family events, but you will find people looking for a compatible partner(s). However, those who attend festivals solely for this purpose will be disappointed and quickly develop a ten-foot-pole reputation.

Attendees don various ritual wear, costumes, and street clothes. Some festivals are clothing-optional; even family-friendly festivals may have a clothing-optional campground for adults. Always check with the presenters before you go skyclad (the witch's word for nude).

Registration for festivals and transportation to the event locations can be costly, particularly if you include camping spots or hotel stays with your registration. An excellent way to explore these gatherings is to attend free Pagan Pride events. These events are worldwide, so you will likely find one near you.

Name	When	Where
Pagan Spirit Gathering (PSG)	June	Missouri
Heartland Pagan Festival	May	Kansas
Pagan Unity Festival (PUF)	May	Tennessee
Starwood Festival	July	Ohio
Sirius Rising	July	New York
Witchfest International	November	London

Monday 22

Earth Day
☽v/c 6:23 pm
Lyrids Meteor Shower

Tuesday 23

○ 6:48 pm
☽♏ 10:20 am
Lyrids Meteor Shower

Wednesday 24

Thursday 25

☿℞ Ends
☽v/c 1:25 pm - ☽♐ 8:37 pm

Friday 26

Saturday 27

Sunday 28

☽v/c 1:56 am - ☽♑ 4:38 am

Beltane

Beltane marks the arrival of summer and is a celebration of the power of life. Fertility, growth, joy, sensuality, and sexuality are central themes of this Sabbat. Here are a few ideas to infuse your Beltane celebration with joy and abundance:

Maypole Dance: Set up a Maypole adorned with colorful ribbons and invite friends and loved ones to participate in the traditional Maypole dance. Weaving the ribbons together celebrates community and the harmonious union of energies.

A print from 1891 shows the Maypole dance. It is entitled "May Day Festivities."

Flower Crowns: Create flower crowns using fresh blooms and foliage. Wear them to embrace your connection with nature.

Bonfires: Light a sacred bonfire and gather around its warm glow, reflecting on gratitude. Write down the things you wish to release and burn the paper in the fire.

Picnics: Enjoy a festive picnic in nature, indulging in seasonal foods and drinks. Surround yourself with the sights, sounds, and scents of the burgeoning Earth.

Sacred Baths: Take a ritual bath infused with flowers, herbs, and essential oils. Cleanse your body, mind, and spirit, invoking the energy of Beltane's passion and vitality.

Offerings to Nature: Express your appreciation for the abundance and beauty of the natural world by creating small offerings of gratitude. Place dishes of birdseed or small bouquets outside while expressing your appreciation for the abundance and beauty of the natural world.

Monday 29

Tuesday 30

✿ Beltane Eve
☽v/c 10:18 am - ☽≈ 10:20 am

Wednesday 1

✿ Beltane
◑ 6:27 am
WitchAcademy.org founded 1996

Thursday 2

☽v/c 4:28 am - ☽✶ 1:52 pm

Friday 3

Saturday 4

Herb Day
⊗ 6:59 pm
☽v/c 7:22 am - ☽♈ 3:41 pm
May the fourth be with you.

Sunday 5

Cinco de Mayo
    International Family Equality Day

May

Mon	Tue	Wed	Thr	Fri	Sat	Sun
		1 ❋◑	2	3	4 ⊗	5
6	7 ●	8	9	10	11	12
13	14	15 ◑	16	17	18	19
20	21	22	23 ○	24	25	26
27	28	29	30 ◑	31		

- National Bike Month
- National Mental Health Awareness Month
- National Stroke Awareness Month

Notes

_____

_____

_____

_____

1	◑	
2	◑	
3	◑	
4	◑	
5	◐	
6	●	
7	●	
8	●	
9	●	
10	◐	
11	◐	
12	◐	
13	◐	
14	◑	
15	◐	
16	◑	
17	◗	
18	○	
19	○	
20	◔	
21	○	
22	○	
23	○	
24	○	
25	○	
26	◔	
27	◑	
28	◑	
29	◑	
30	◑	
31	◑	

Yarrow Magic

The International Herb Association selects one herb yearly to be celebrated during the week before Mother's Day. For 2024, the featured herb is yarrow (*Achillea millefolium*). While nurseries and popular media focus on its uses in the garden, witches may revel in its magical properties.

Protection and Boundaries:
Yarrow shields from magical attacks and negative energies. It can also boost your courage, allowing you to stick firmly to your boundaries. Harness this power by incorporating the herb into spell bottles, wreaths, altar bouquets, spell bags, and talismans.

Divination: Yarrow amplifies intuition and psychic abilities. Bundles of the stalks are used in I Ching[4] divination, and witches sometimes store small bundles of the herb with tarot and oracle cards or other divinatory tools.

Healing: Yarrow aids in emotional healing, helping to mend broken hearts and bring balance to the body and mind. The herb can aid this purpose when used in sachets or dream pillows. Use it in incense, either alone over an incense charcoal or combined with resins such as frankincense.

Love Magic: Yarrow fosters self-love and acceptance, attracts romance, and deepens existing relationships' connections.

Ritual Offerings: To use as an offering in rituals and ceremonies, burn the dried herb to the deities, spirits, or ancestors, invoking their blessings and guidance. It is popular in altar bouquets for Beltane and Midsummer and on altars dedicated to the goddess Hestia.

Monday 6

National Nurses Day
☽v/c 12:56 am - ☽♉ 4:42 pm
Eta Aquarids Meteor Shower

Tuesday 7

● 10:21 pm
Eta Aquarids Meteor Shower

Wednesday 8

☽v/c 11:30 am - ☽♊ 6:21 pm

Thursday 9

Friday 10

☽v/c 12:12 pm - ☽♋ 10:13 pm

Saturday 11

Sunday 12

Mother's Day
☽v/c 11:56 pm
International Nurses Day

Honoring Elders

In this sacred space, we gather near,
To honor elders, those we hold dear.
With hearts open wide, we come together,
To keep their wisdom, now and forever.

We call upon the elders, both near and far,
Guiding lights, like twinkling stars.
Their journeys paved with love and pride,
Through struggles faced, they've stood beside.

With reverence, we honor your shining light,
For the courage you've shown in your fight.
You've paved the way, shattered walls with grace,
with dignity and love, in every vibrant embrace.

Through trials and triumphs, you've stood tall,
Championing equality for one and all.
Your stories, like ancient wisdom, unfold,
A tapestry of resilience, vibrant and bold.

We honor those who blazed the trail,
Our wise elders who refused to fail.
Their strength and courage, an inspiration,
Their stories echo through generations.

With reverence we hold them in our sight,
Their wisdom shining like a beacon bright.
They've weathered storms, fought for their rights,
Their voices echo through endless nights.

Blessings upon you with each passing day,
May joy and peace forever come your way.
In our hearts, your spirits shall reside,
With love and respect, by your side.

So, we invoke this sacred blessing tonight,
For elders of our community, shining bright.
May your spirits soar like rainbows in the sky,
May your wisdom be cherished as time goes by.

Monday 13

☽ ♌ 5:36 am

Tuesday 14

Wednesday 15

◑ 6:48 am
☽ v/c 11:40 am - ☽ ♍ 4:33 pm

Thursday 16

National Honor Our LGBT Elders Day

Friday 17

Malcolm X Day

Saturday 18

☽ v/c 1:41 am - ☽ ♎ 5:23 am

Sunday 19

☽ v/c 10:48 am

Prosperity Pasta

This spell demonstrates the enchantment of modern kitchen witchcraft, merging the culinary arts with magic to explore new dimensions of your witchy path. Kitchen witchery often incorporates herbs and crystals to harness the energies of the natural world, as seen in this recipe/spell.

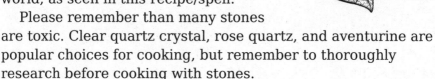

Basil

Please remember than many stones are toxic. Clear quartz crystal, rose quartz, and aventurine are popular choices for cooking, but remember to thoroughly research before cooking with stones.

Ingredients:

- Green aventurine stone, tumble polished, thoroughly washed[5] (for abundance and prosperity)
- Basil leaves, fresh (wealth and success)
- Your favorite pasta (abundance)
- Salt (purification of the meal)
- Olive oil (wisdom and abundance)
- Garlic, fresh or powder (protects from financial drain)

Instructions:

- Ground yourself and set your intention. Visualize abundance and prosperity flowing into your life.
- Prepare your pasta as you usually would in boiling salted water. When you add the salt, focus on pushing out anything baneful that will interfere with your intention.
- Hold the aventurine in your hands as the pasta cooks, infusing it with your intentions. Add the stone to your boiling pasta.
- When your pasta is cooked, drain it and remove the aventurine. Drizzle olive oil over the pasta as you visualize prosperity flowing into your life. Start with a tablespoon and adjust to your taste. Continue your focus and visualization while you add basil, garlic, and salt.

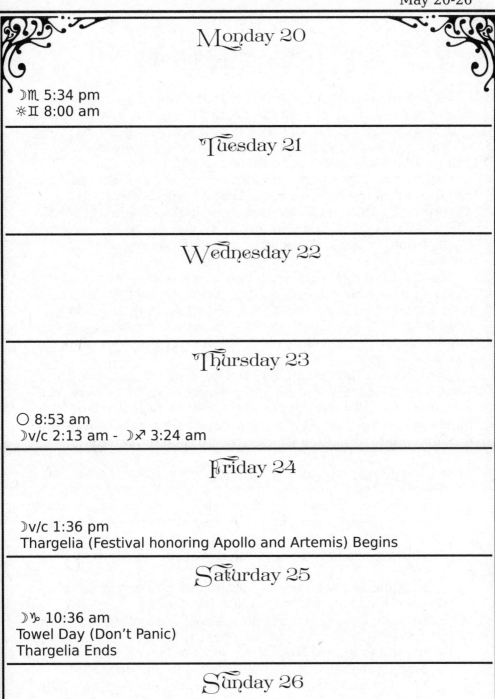

Monday 20

☽♏ 5:34 pm
☼♊ 8:00 am

Tuesday 21

Wednesday 22

Thursday 23

○ 8:53 am
☽v/c 2:13 am - ☽♐ 3:24 am

Friday 24

☽v/c 1:36 pm
Thargelia (Festival honoring Apollo and Artemis) Begins

Saturday 25

☽♑ 10:36 am
Towel Day (Don't Panic)
Thargelia Ends

Sunday 26

☽v/c 10:36 pm

Earthing Rituals

This week, National Go Barefoot Day gives us an excellent opportunity to connect with the Earth's energy. In a world filled with constant busyness and technological distractions, earthing rituals provide an opportunity to find solace, restore balance, and establish a deeper connection with nature.

Earthing and grounding rituals are very similar, but earthing rituals tend to focus on a physical connection to the Earth. Theoretically, this physical connection neutralizes the positively charged ions that accumulate in our bodies due to our proximity to electronic devices and other sources of electromagnetic radiation.

Static grounding is another element associated with earthing rituals. Our bodies can accumulate static electricity from various sources, such as synthetic materials, carpeted floors, and electronic equipment. Earthing practices create an opportunity to discharge this static electricity and restore our natural electrical balance.

Earthing is a trendy catchphrase for a variety of snake-oil sales tactics. Many scientific and pseudo-scientific devices, such as grounding mats and copper socks, can be purchased at highly inflated prices. And yet, you can easily incorporate static grounding into any ritual free of charge (pun intended).

- To incorporate static grounding into a ritual, find a suitable outdoor space. Remove your shoes and socks to establish a direct connection with the Earth. Stand or sit on the ground, ensuring that your bare feet or body come into contact with the Earth's surface. You can press your palms down onto the ground if you don't wish to go barefoot.
- Imagine any accumulated static charge flowing out of your body and dissipating into the ground.
- Breathe deeply, visualizing yourself being anchored to the Earth, feeling its supportive energy.
- Stand tall and stretch. Then begin to slowly walk barefoot, allowing each step to be mindful and deliberate. Feel the texture of the Earth beneath your feet, whether it's cool grass, soft sand, or uneven forest floor. As you walk, visualize any stress or negativity being absorbed by the Earth, transforming into positive energy.
- You can end your earthing exercise now or continue with meditation or any other ritual.

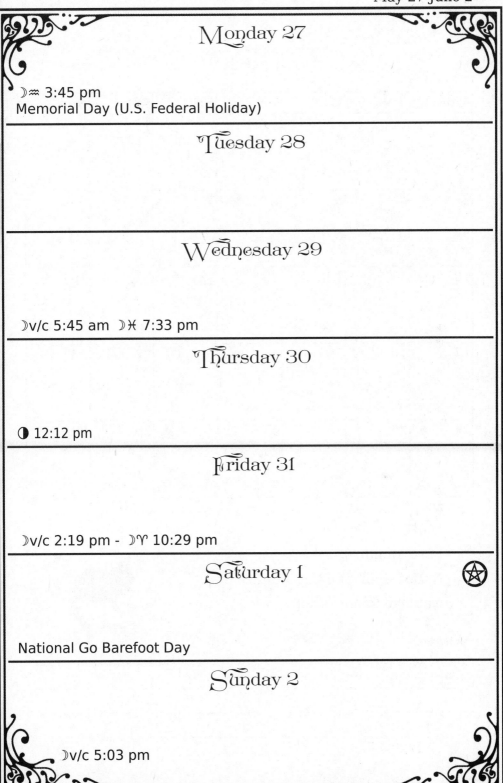

Monday 27

☽♒ 3:45 pm
Memorial Day (U.S. Federal Holiday)

Tuesday 28

Wednesday 29

☽v/c 5:45 am ☽♓ 7:33 pm

Thursday 30

◑ 12:12 pm

Friday 31

☽v/c 2:19 pm - ☽♈ 10:29 pm

Saturday 1

⛤

National Go Barefoot Day

Sunday 2

☽v/c 5:03 pm

June

Mon	Tue	Wed	Thr	Fri	Sat	Sun
					1	2
3	4	5	6 ●	7	8	9
10	11	12	13	14 ◗	15	16
17	18	19	20 ❊	21 ○	22	23
24	25	26	27	28 ◖	29	30

- LGBTQIA+ Pride Month
- Rose Month
- National Adopt a Cat Month
- National Candy Month

Notes

_____

_____

_____

_____

1	
2	
3	
4	
5	
6	
7	
8	
9	
10	
11	
12	
13	
14	
15	
16	
17	
18	
19	
20	
21	
22	
23	
24	
25	
26	
27	
28	
29	
30	

Bottle Binding Magic

Bottle spells are surging in popularity. Like the classic spell pouch, bottle spells harness the powers of herbs, crystals, and other natural ingredients to help focus your intentions. Instructions for making these charms can be found in the December articles.

While picking up trash on a walk in the woods, I was inspired by a discarded bottle entangled in woodbine. I realized that binding bottles with a living vine could seal and add power to spell bottles. Vine-bound spell bottles incorporate the plant's energy into your work and help with anchoring and manifesting your magic.

The first plant I used for this technique was morning glory vines. They remain my favorite plant choice because they bind bottles quickly. However, their growing season is limited because they are outdoor summer annuals. English Ivy grows indoors and outdoors, but it will take longer to bind your bottle. Next week's article has suggestions for various vines.

Instructions

• Select a bottle with a shape that will support the vine as it grows. Cylindrical bottles may slip out of the vines, whereas a bottle with a narrower neck and broader base can work well. You can use a spell bottle you have already created or use an empty bottle for future spellwork.

• Choose a vine plant that is suitable for your growing conditions with a climbing or trailing habit.

• Hang a small bottle next to the vine of your choice. I prefer to hang mine on small hooks near the tips of the vine.

• Check on it once or twice a week and encourage vines to grow around it. Guide the vine's growth by gently training it to wrap around the bottle. You can use soft plant ties or twisty ties to secure the vine to the bottle at various points as it grows.

• When the bottle is bound, thank the plant for its service. Detach the bottle with clippers and allow the vine to dry on the bottle in a cool, dry area.

Monday 3

☽♉ 12:56 am
World Bicycle Day

Tuesday 4

☽v/c 8:45 am

Wednesday 5

☽♊ 3:36 am
World Environment Day

Thursday 6

● 7:37 am

Friday 7

☽v/c 5:21 am - ☽♋ 7:41 am
Vestalia (Festival of Vesta/Hestia) Begins

Saturday 8

☽v/c 6:07 pm
World Oceans Day

Sunday 9

☽♌ 2:29 pm

Vining Plant Magic

Vines enhance your connection with nature and symbolize growth, resilience, and expansion. Incorporate this symbolism into personal development, abundance, and manifestation spells.

Vines are versatile tools for rituals and magic. Their intertwining quality makes them ideal for binding spells. Wrap dried or living vines around a representation of something you wish to bind. Vines are also protective; you can fashion them into a wreath to ward off negative energy or unwanted influences. You can create a vine talisman by braiding or knotting vines and carrying it as a protective charm. Ivy, honeysuckle, grape, and trumpet vines are used instead of the traditional cords in handfasting rituals.

You can use any vine for any magical purpose or select one with correspondences aligned with your spellwork. These suggestions are listed in my order of preference for binding spell bottles, as detailed in last week's article.

Morning Glory (*Ipomoea* spp.) — outdoor vine used for magical and psychic power, insight, peace, and joy.

Green Beans (*Phaseolus vulgaris*) — a popular garden vegetable used for prosperity, fertility, and abundance.

Clematis (*Clematis* spp.) — grown outdoors and used for wisdom, travel, and perseverance.

Wisteria (*Wisteria* spp.) — a woody outdoor vine used for healing, stress relief, wisdom, and love.

Grape Vine (*Vitis* spp.) — used for any purpose, especially celebration, joy, protection, abundance, healing, and growth.

Trumpet Vine (*Campsis radicans*) — an outdoor vine used for courage, victory, strength, confidence, and celebration.

Kiwi Vine (*Actinidia* spp.) — an outdoor fruit crop vine used for fertility, protection, love, attraction, joy, and healing.

Honeysuckle (*Lonicera* spp.) — a summer perennial used for love, protection, generosity, beauty, and purification.

English Ivy (*Hedera helix*) — can be grown indoors or outside in many climates. It is associated with sexuality, pleasure, lust, protection, binding, and growth.

Pothos (*Epipremnum aureum*) — an easy-to-grow houseplant used for protection, luck, prosperity, resiliency, and adaptability.

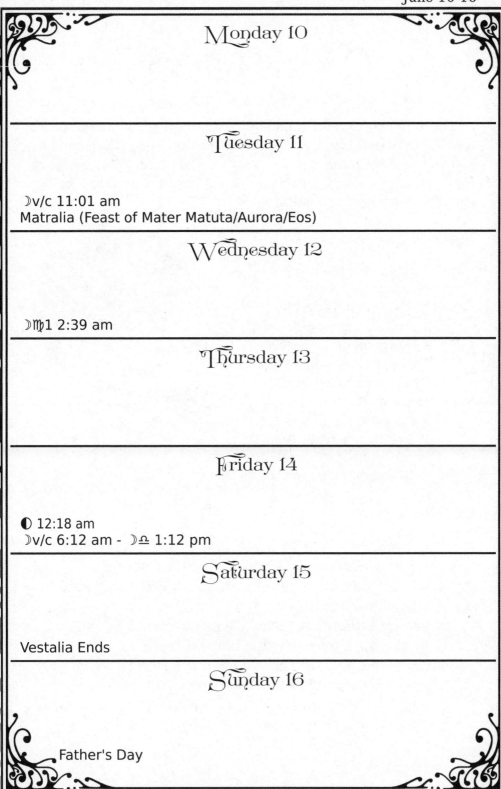

Monday 10

Tuesday 11

☽v/c 11:01 am
Matralia (Feast of Mater Matuta/Aurora/Eos)

Wednesday 12

☽♍1 2:39 am

Thursday 13

Friday 14

☽ 12:18 am
☽v/c 6:12 am - ☽♎ 1:12 pm

Saturday 15

Vestalia Ends

Sunday 16

Father's Day

Garden Herb Dip

This dip incorporates the magical energies of healing and protective herbs. It is a perfect treat for the season, and can be enjoyed with crudités, chips, crackers, and salads. This recipe is for dried herbs, but you may double the amount required for each fresh herb you substitute.

Ingredients

- 1 cup sour cream
- ½ cup mayonnaise
- 1 tablespoon lemon juice
- 1 teaspoon dried dill
- 1 teaspoon dried parsley
- 1 teaspoon dried chives
- 1 teaspoon dried basil
- ½ teaspoon dried thyme
- 1 teaspoon dried rosemary
- ½ teaspoon dried oregano
- ½ teaspoon garlic powder
- Salt and black pepper to taste

Instructions

1. In a medium-sized bowl, combine the sour cream, mayonnaise, and lemon juice. Mix well until smooth.
2. Add the remaining ingredients and stir to incorporate everything evenly.
3. Season with salt and black pepper according to your taste. Adjust the amount of herbs if desired.
4. Cover the bowl with plastic wrap and refrigerate for at least 1 hour to allow the flavors to meld together.
5. Before serving, give the dip a good stir. Taste and adjust the seasoning if necessary.

Monday 17

☽v/c 1:04 am - ☽♏ 1:38 am

Tuesday 18

☽v/c 3:18 pm

Wednesday 19

☽♐ 11:32 am
Juneteenth (U.S. Federal Holiday)

Thursday 20

☼♋ 3:50 pm
☽v/c 11:07 pm
❀ Midsummer 3:50 pm

Friday 21

○ 8:07 pm
☽♑ 6:09 pm
International Day of Yoga

Saturday 22

Sunday 23

☽v/c 4:01 am - ☽♒ 10:15 pm

Midsummer

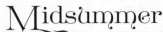

We celebrate the height of summer on this solstice Sabbat. Midsummer is also known as Litha, and it is known as a time when connecting with nature spirits is more accessible. Here are a few ideas to infuse your celebrations with magic and joy:

Herbs & Flowers: This is the perfect time to gather and harvest herbs at their peak potency. Make fresh tinctures or dry the herbs for later use. Create a flower mandala or sun wheel with fresh blossoms, using it as an offering, altar decoration, or a focus for meditation. Sunflowers, calendula, and chamomile are associated with the season.

Sunrise or Sunset Meditation: Find a serene location to witness the sunrise or sunset on the solstice. Meditate and reflect on the Sun's energy and its impact on your life or set intentions for the remainder of the year. Yoga practitioners will enjoy greeting the day with the classic sun salutation.

Sun Magnification: Harness the energy of the Sun with a magnifying glass, using it to light ritual fires, incense, herb bundles, or smoking pipes.

Drum Circle: Gather friends and create a drum circle, celebrating summer's rhythm and life's vitality. Drumming and dancing together in sync can generate powerful energy and connections.

Solar Foods and Drinks: Prepare a feast featuring foods associated with the Sun, such as citrus fruits, honey, sun-dried tomatoes, and yellow or orange vegetables. Enjoy refreshing beverages infused with citrus or herbs.

Monday 24

☽v/c 5:58 pm
Festival of Fortuna/Tyche

Tuesday 25

Wednesday 26

⬟

☽⬧ 1:08 am

Thursday 27

☽v/c 1:10 pm

Friday 28

☽ 4:53 pm
☽♈ 3:52 am

Saturday 29

☽v/c 11:56 pm

Sunday 30

☽♉ 7:01 am

July

Mon	Tue	Wed	Thr	Fri	Sat	Sun
1	2	3	4	5 ●	6	7
8	9	10	11	12	13 ◐	14
15	16	17	18	19	20	21 ○
22	23	24	25	26	27 ◑	28
29	30	31				

- Disability Pride Month
- National Ice Cream Month
- National Picnic Month

Notes

_____

_____

_____

_____

_____

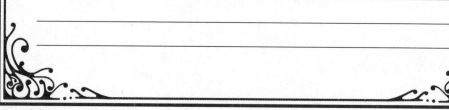

1	
2	
3	
4	
5	
6	
7	
8	
9	
10	
11	
12	
13	
14	
15	
16	
17	
18	
19	
20	
21	
22	
23	
24	
25	
26	
27	
28	
29	
30	
31	

Humor Nourishes Spirit

Laughter releases tension, uplifts our spirits, and fosters connection. Through humor, we gain perspective and learn to find lightness amidst life's challenges. It enables us to navigate difficulties with grace and resilience. Embrace humor to create space for joy and cultivate a deeper understanding of yourself and the world around you, ultimately nurturing your spiritual journey toward greater self-discovery and enlightenment. Try to bring some humor into your life this week. You might see a comedy movie, listen to a funny podcast, or peruse my terrible herb and garden jokes.

- What did the parsley say to the basil?
  "You're kind of a big dill!"
- Why did the oregano blush?
  It saw the salad dressing!
- Why did the herb win the race?
  It had a lot of thyme on its side!
- How did the herb escape from jail?
  It used a little dill-usion!
- How do herbs celebrate Halloween?
  They have a bewitching thyme!
- How do herbs travel?
  They use thyme-travel.
- Why was the mint so good at telling jokes?
  It had a refreshing sense of humor!
- Why did the herb take up meditation?
  It wanted to find inner peas!
- What's an herb's favorite type of dance?
  The salsa!
- Why did they break up with their garden?
  They were always getting jalapeño business!
- Why did the herb go to the art gallery?
  It wanted to see some herb-stract paintings!
- How do herbs counsel each other?
  With sage advice!

Monday 1

☽v/c 4:27 pm
International Joke Day

Tuesday 2

☽♊ 10:50 am

Wednesday 3

☽v/c 8:57 pm

Thursday 4

☽♋c 3:52 pm
Independence Day (U.S. Federal Holiday)

Friday 5

● 5:57 pm

Saturday 6

☽v/c 11:26 am - ☽♌ 10:56 pm

Sunday 7

World Chocolate Day

Oil Infusions & Ointments

Making ointment is a rewarding and empowering process allowing you to harness the magical and healing properties of herbs and oils.

Ingredients

1 cup of carrier oil
1/4 cup of <u>dried</u> herbs
1/4 cup of grated beeswax

Directions

1. Choose herbs that align with your intended purpose, such as lavender for relaxation or calendula for soothing skin.
2. Place your chosen herbs in a jar and cover them with a carrier oil (such as olive or jojoba oil). Seal the jar and let it sit for several weeks in a cool dark place. Shake the jar occasionally to aid in extraction.
3. After the infusion period, strain the oil using cheesecloth or a fine-mesh sieve to remove the herb particles.
4. In a double boiler, gently melt the beeswax until it becomes liquid.
5. Slowly pour the infused oil into the melted beeswax while stirring continuously. Mix thoroughly to ensure a homogeneous blend.
6. Carefully pour the warm mixture into clean, sterilized containers. Allow it to cool and solidify completely before sealing.

Lip Balm

Lip balm is an ointment with a firm texture. Use the same technique as above, but change the quantities thusly:

1 tablespoon beeswax pellets or grated beeswax
1 tablespoon oil (infused oil or your choice of carrier oil)
1 tablespoon shea butter
Optional: 6 drops of peppermint essential oil

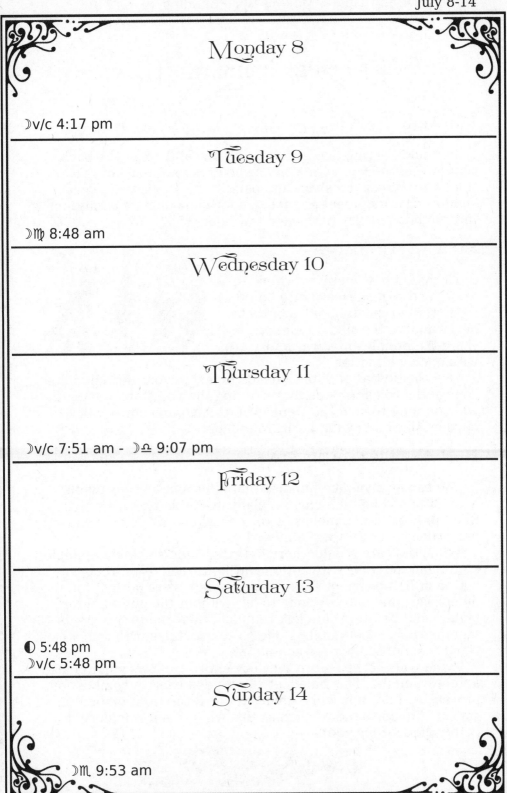

Monday 8

☽v/c 4:17 pm

Tuesday 9

☽♍ 8:48 am

Wednesday 10

Thursday 11

☽v/c 7:51 am - ☽♎ 9:07 pm

Friday 12

Saturday 13

☽ 5:48 pm
☽v/c 5:48 pm

Sunday 14

☽♏ 9:53 am

Harvest Drying Tips

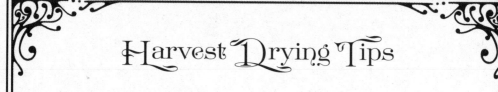

Flower & Leaves

For quick drying, select a hot, dry day and cover the back seat of your vehicle with a clean sheet. Strew your herbs in a thin layer across the sheet and park in the shade with each window cracked about an inch. Under ideal climate conditions, this method can dry herbs in a few hours.

Stems & Branches

Herbs such as mugwort, wormwood, and rosemary are dried on the stem. Gather small bundles of these herbs and tie the stems together. Hang the bundles in a warm, dry area with good ventilation.

Use elastic ties or rubber bands to fasten your herb bundles. Your herbs will shrink as they dry, and the adjustable fasteners will continue to hold the stems while string and cords will become slack, allowing herbs to escape.

Herb Bundles for Incense

You can easily make bundles that offer a more reasonable amount of smoke than commercially available types. Harvest the top three to five inches of your chosen herb's stems and hang them until they are almost dry.

While they are still leathery in texture and somewhat pliable, bind them together with cotton sewing thread or untreated cotton or hemp string. Thumb-sized bundles are perfect for indoor use, and will continue to dry without the potential for mold found in fatter bundles. You must tie three to five stalks together for proper combustion, so select stalks with thin stems. Hang them until they are completely dry.

Tying your herbs before they dry entirely allows you to make a tighter bundle. This balances the oxygen used in combustion, preventing flare-ups while giving you just the right amount of smoke. Smaller bundles such as this will remain smoldering better than larger bundles.

Monday 15

Tuesday 16

☽v/c 3:05 pm - ☽✗ 10:25 pm

Wednesday 17

Thursday 18

☽v/c 3:23 pm

Friday 19

☽♑ 3:14 am

Saturday 20

Sunday 21

○ 5:17 am
☽v/c 5:16 am - ☽♒ 6:43 am

Tinctures

Tinctures are concentrated liquid extracts made from herbs or other plant materials. This traditional method of herbal medicine has been used for centuries to create extracts known for their long shelf life, often lasting several years when stored properly.

To make a tincture, you'll need a combination of dried herbs or plant parts and high-proof alcohol, such as vodka, rum, or grain alcohol. The alcohol acts as a solvent, extracting the beneficial compounds from the plants. Try the following recipe with herbs associated with purification. I like to use rosemary, sage, and eucalyptus. Use your tincture to clear your home by filling a spray bottle with water and adding a few drops of tincture.

Ingredients

- 1 cup dried herbs or plant material
- 2 cups high-proof, food-safe alcohol (e.g., vodka, rum, or grain alcohol)

Instructions

1. Place the dried herbs or plant material in a glass jar and pour the alcohol over them until completely covered. You may add more or less alcohol than listed in the ingredients as necessary. Seal the jar tightly and shake it.
2. Store the jar in a cool, dark place, and let the mixture infuse for about 4 to 6 weeks, shaking it periodically.
3. After the infusion period, strain the liquid through a fine-mesh sieve or cheesecloth, squeezing out as much liquid as possible.

   3a. Optional: For concentrated tinctures, return the liquid to the jar with more dried herbs, infusing as before.

4. Transfer the tincture into amber glass bottles with droppers for easy use and storage. Label the bottles with the name of the tincture, the ingredients, and the date of preparation.

   Remember to research the specific herb you're using for any precautions or dosage recommendations.

Monday 22

☀ ♌ 2:45 am

Tuesday 23

☽v/c 4:57 pm - ☽⠙ 8:23 am

Wednesday 24

☽v/c 3:31 pm

Thursday 25   ⛤

☽♈ 9:53 am

Friday 26

☽v/c 5:14 pm

Saturday 27

◑ 9:51 pm
☽♉ 12:23 pm

Sunday 28

Parents' Day
Delta Aquarids Meteor Shower

Lughnasadh

Lughnasadh, also known as Lammas, celebrates the first harvest and the abundance of the Earth. This Sabbat marks the transition from summer to autumn. We reap the harvest of the projects we began in the spring, enjoying the bountiful harvest with gratitude. Here are a few ideas for your celebrations:

Harvest Ritual: Gather the first fruits, vegetables, or grains from your garden or local farmers' market. Offer thanks to the Earth and deities for the abundance of the harvest. Share the bounty with others through donations or a communal feast.

Baking Bread: Honor the harvest by baking a loaf of home-made bread using locally sourced grains. Incorporate herbs and seeds representing abundance and prosperity. Share the bread with loved ones, offering them the sustenance of the season.

Outdoor Games: Organize activities to celebrate the spirit of competition and skill, reminiscent of the ancient Lughnasadh fairs. Engage in friendly contests such as sack races, tug of war, or archery.

Crafting: Embrace the spirit of Lugh, the skilled craftsman, by creating something beautiful and meaningful with your hands. Practice crafting skills such as weaving, pottery, candle making, or woodworking. Make some teas, infused oils, or other herbal crafts, or create corn dollies using dried corn husks and use them as decorations or offerings.

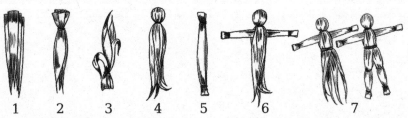

1   2   3   4   5   6   7

To make corn dollies, soak corn husks in warm water for half and hour and then (1) gather a small bundle of husks, (2) tie one end with strips of corn husk or rubber bands, (3) pull the long ends of husks down over the tie, (4) tie the husks again under the ball created in the previous step, (5) fold a husk into a thin strip and tie the ends, (6) insert the thin strip through the dolly to create arms, (7) tie around the dolly's waist and optionally tie pants.

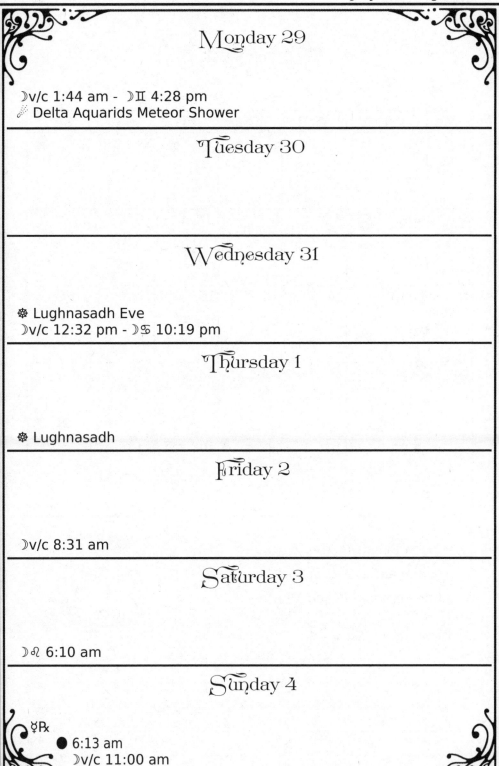

Monday 29

☽v/c 1:44 am - ☽♊ 4:28 pm
☄ Delta Aquarids Meteor Shower

Tuesday 30

Wednesday 31

❀ Lughnasadh Eve
☽v/c 12:32 pm - ☽♋ 10:19 pm

Thursday 1

❀ Lughnasadh

Friday 2

☽v/c 8:31 am

Saturday 3

☽♌ 6:10 am

Sunday 4

☿℞
● 6:13 am
☽v/c 11:00 am

August

Mon	Tue	Wed	Thr	Fri	Sat	Sun
			1 ⛢	2 ⛢	3	4 ● ☿℞
5	6 ⊗	7	8	9	10	11
12 ◐	13	14	15	16	17	18
19 ○	20	21	22	23	24	25
26 ◑	27	28 ☿℞ Ends	29	30	31	

- Black Business Month
- National Back to School Month
- International Peace Month

Notes

_____

_____

_____

_____

1	
2	
3	
4	
5	
6	
7	
8	
9	
10	
11	
12	
13	
14	
15	
16	
17	
18	
19	
20	
21	
22	
23	
24	
25	
26	
27	
28	
29	
30	
31	

Learning Runes

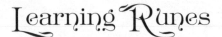

Using runes for divination is an ancient practice that taps into the wisdom of the Norse gods and the runic alphabet. Here's a brief guide on how to use runes for divination:

1. Acquire a rune set: Obtain a set of rune stones or create your own by inscribing the runic symbols onto small stones or wooden pieces. The traditional Elder Futhark consists of 24 runes.

2. Set your intention: Before each reading, focus your mind and clarify your intention or question. This helps create a clear energy for the divination process.

3. Draw runes: Randomly draw a set number of runes from the bag or pile while concentrating on your question. The number of runes drawn can vary depending on the complexity of the question or the spread you choose.

4. Interpret the runes: Study the symbols drawn and their meanings. Each rune carries its own significance, representing aspects of life, challenges, opportunities, or guidance. Interpret the combination of runes and their positions in relation to your question.

5. Trust your intuition: Allow your intuition to guide your interpretation of the runes. Pay attention to any feelings, thoughts, or insights that arise during the process. Trust your inner wisdom and the messages conveyed through the runes.

6. Reflect and take action: Reflect on the messages received and consider how they relate to your situation. Use the insights gained to make informed decisions or take necessary actions in your life.

Rune divination is a tool for self-reflection and guidance. Approach it with respect, reverence, and an open mind. With practice, the ancient wisdom of the runes can provide valuable insights and support on your life's journey.

Monday 5

☽♍ 4:17 pm

Tuesday 6

⊗ 7:00 pm

Wednesday 7

☽v/c 4:43 am

Thursday 8

☽♎ 4:32 am

Friday 9

☽v/c 4:44 pm

Saturday 10

☽♏ 5:34 pm

Sunday 11

Nemoralia

Nemoralia is an ancient Roman festival held from August 13th through the 15th. It is an occasion dedicated to the worship of the goddess Diana. She is known for her association with the hunt and the wilderness. This celebration also offers a fascinating glimpse into the cross-cultural connections between Roman and Greek mythology, as Diana finds her counterpart in the Greek goddess Artemis.

Artemis, the daughter of Zeus and Leto, shares many similarities with Diana. Both goddesses are renowned for their affinity with the natural world, archery skill, and status as protectors of women and childbirth. They embody the strength, independence, and untamed spirit often associated with female divinity.

While Diana holds prominence in Roman mythology, Artemis occupies a similar role in Greek mythology. As the patroness of the

16th century engraving of Diana the huntress acompanied by her dogs.

hunt, Artemis is revered as a goddess of the wilderness and protector of animals. She is often depicted with a bow and arrows, and her temples were sanctuaries for those seeking her favor and guidance.

The festival of Nemoralia pays tribute to the Roman reverence for Diana, but its origins and symbolism draw from the deeper well of ancient beliefs that transcend geographical boundaries. It is a testament to the shared cultural heritage and the interconnectedness of Roman and Greek mythologies. Nemoralia is an ancient tradition that continues to inspire and captivate us today.

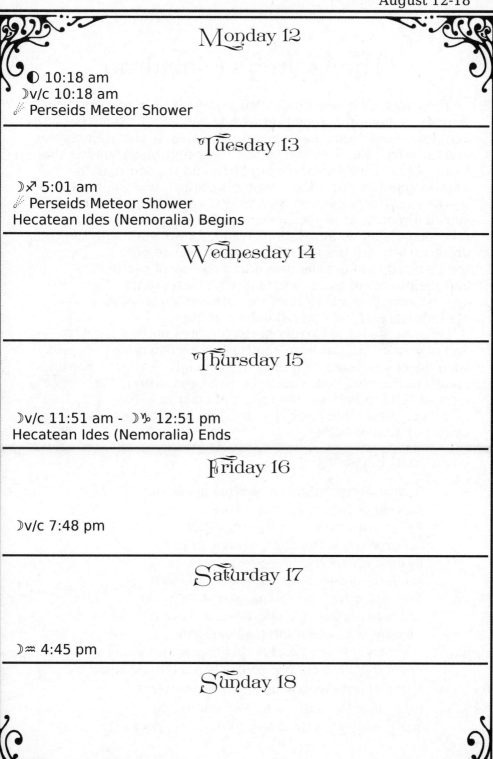

Monday 12

◑ 10:18 am
☽v/c 10:18 am
☄ Perseids Meteor Shower

Tuesday 13

☽♐ 5:01 am
☄ Perseids Meteor Shower
Hecatean Ides (Nemoralia) Begins

Wednesday 14

Thursday 15

☽v/c 11:51 am - ☽♑ 12:51 pm
Hecatean Ides (Nemoralia) Ends

Friday 16

☽v/c 7:48 pm

Saturday 17

☽♒ 4:45 pm

Sunday 18

The Witch's Cauldron

The cauldron holds a profound significance in our practices. With its elemental association with water, it represents the ebb and flow of emotions, healing, and intuition. It also reflects the unity of earth, air, fire, and water. The cauldron's rounded shape resembles a womb, symbolizing birth and transformation. Three-legged cauldrons are symbols of the triple Goddess.

The cauldron serves as a portal between the physical and spiritual realms. It is a space where intentions are set, dreams take shape, and manifestations occur. As we work with the cauldron, we tap into the transformative power of fire, the inspiration of air, the grounding energy of earth, and the fluidity of water, aligning with the essence of existence. It reminds us of the interconnectedness of all things and the cyclical nature of life.

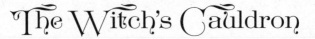

Use your cauldron to mix herbs for spell bottles and pouches. You can burn spells you've written on small pieces of paper to release their magic for manifestation. Fill your cauldron with sand, using colored sand to harness the magic of color association. Your sand-filled cauldron can then be used as a censer or candle holder.

Cauldron Blessing

In this sacred hour, I consecrate anew,
Blessed cauldron, pure and true.
By fire's warmth and flickering light,
I charge you with magic, shining bright.
By air's whispers and gentle breeze,
You'll carry intentions with graceful ease.
Through earth's grounding and stability,
You hold the essence of divine ability.
By water's flow and intuitive embrace,
You'll magnify energies in this sacred space.
From this moment on, you're blessed and sealed,
A vessel of power, your essence revealed.
Infused with magic, a sacred embrace,
Your potential unleashed, filling this space.

Monday 19

☽v/c 1:25 pm - ☽♓ 5:52 pm
○ 1:25 pm (Seasonal Blue Moon)

Tuesday 20

Wednesday 21

☽v/c 3:33 am - ☽♈ 6:02 pm

Thursday 22

☀♍ 9:55 am

Friday 23

☽v/c 7:44 am - ☽♉ 7:01 pm

Saturday 24

Sunday 25

☽v/c 2:02 pm - ☽♊ 10:04 pm

Winnowing for Witches

Two women winnowing sesame in South Korea

Winnowing is a simple yet effective technique used to separate grain from its chaff or, in a broader sense, to separate the valuable from the unwanted. This method has been employed for centuries in agriculture and has now found its way into various other domains.

Many witches fill their cauldrons with sand for use as a censer or candle holder. Winnowing this sand will remove ashes, bits of wax, and the sticks used to support incense. You'll want to do your winnowing on a day with a light breeze. Sift out large bits of debris by pouring the sand through a colander. Select two large bowls and pour the sifted sand into one.

Take both bowls outdoors and hold the bowl of sand over the second bowl, slowly tip out the sand. Let the gentle breeze carry away the ashes and lighter bits of herbs and incense remnants. The cleaned sand should land in your second dish. Hold the two bowls closer together or wait for a day with less wind if your sand is scattering about. Repeat the winnowing process until your sand is suitably clean. You can do this witchy housekeeping in less than a minute with practice and patience.

Monday 26

◐ 4:25 am
Women's Equality Day

Tuesday 27

Wednesday 28

☿℞ Ends
☽v/c 12:50 am - ☽♋ 3:48 am

Thursday 29

☽v/c 10:57 am

Friday 30

☽♌ 12:10 am

Saturday 31

Sunday 1

☽v/c 7:24 pm - ☽♍ 10:49 pm

September

Mon	Tue	Wed	Thr	Fri	Sat	Sun
						1
2 ●	3	4	5	6	7	8
9	10	11 ◑	12	13	14	15
16	17 ○	18	19	20	21	22 ✿
23	24 ◐	25	26	27	28	29
30						

- National Mushroom Month
- Self Improvement Month

Notes

1	
2	
3	
4	
5	
6	
7	
8	
9	
10	
11	
12	
13	
14	
15	
16	
17	
18	
19	
20	
21	
22	
23	
24	
25	
26	
27	
28	
29	
30	

Social Justice Witchcraft

Witchcraft as a tool for social justice demonstrates the transformative potential of blending spirituality with activism, reminding us of the inherent power we hold to shape a better world. Witches often engage in shadow work, addressing personal biases and privileges while actively challenging systemic injustices. The craft has long been intertwined with concepts of personal empowerment, embracing diversity, and challenging societal norms.

In 1899 Charles Godfrey Leland published *Aradia, or the Gospel of the Witches*. This book was highly influential in the development of modern Paganism and witchcraft. The first page of chapter one reads, "The rich made slaves of all the poor." and goes on to share an invocation that includes "thou shalt bind the spirit of the oppressor." Later in the same invocation, we read, "Ye who are poor suffer with hunger keen, And toll in wretchedness... ill the fate of all who do ye wrong!"

An increasing number of contemporary witches have been using their craft as a platform for social justice. We understand that by harnessing our power, we can advocate for equality, liberation, and dismantling oppressive systems. Blending activism with rituals and spellwork, we challenge systemic inequalities to foster a more equitable society. Like other systems found in nature, we recognize that various forms of oppression, such as racism, sexism, homophobia, and transphobia, are intertwined and must be addressed collectively.

Many witches actively advocate for inclusivity, equality, and amplifying marginalized voices within their communities and beyond. Personal and collective healing combine to dismantle oppressive structures and create healing spaces for others.

Imagine you are about to join a peaceful protest, and before it starts, you wish to focus your energy on protecting yourself and other protesters. What prayer or invocation might you create for this purpose?

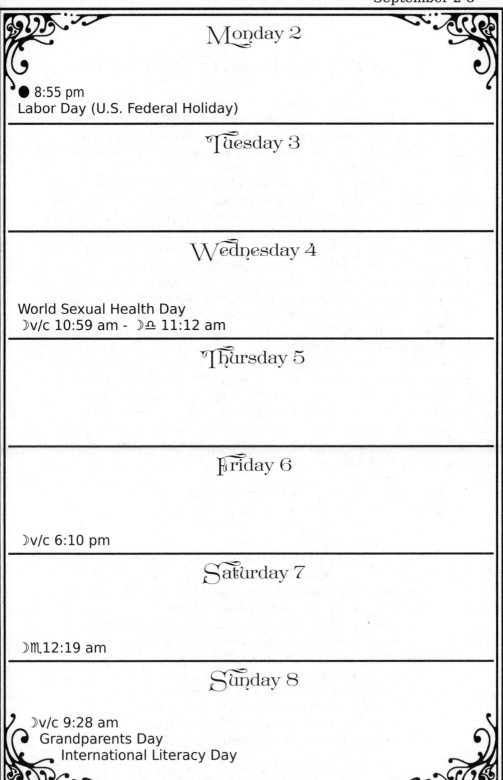

Monday 2

● 8:55 pm
Labor Day (U.S. Federal Holiday)

Tuesday 3

Wednesday 4

World Sexual Health Day
☽v/c 10:59 am - ☽♎ 11:12 am

Thursday 5

Friday 6

☽v/c 6:10 pm

Saturday 7

☽♏ 12:19 am

Sunday 8

☽v/c 9:28 am
  Grandparents Day
    International Literacy Day

Embracing Love & Pleasure

One of the most renowned invocations in witchcraft, the Charge of the Goddess, holds a significant place within the practice. This sacred poem explicitly states that witches do not partake in sacrifices, emphasizing that acts of love and pleasure serve as rituals of the goddess.

In contrast to the cultural narrative of sacrifice prevalent in Abrahamic faiths, witchcraft offers an alternative perspective that values individual freedom and self-expression. It acknowledges that each person has the right to pursue their desires without causing harm to others. This distinction highlights the unique ethos of witchcraft, empowering practitioners to honor and celebrate life's joys. The Charge declares that all acts driven by love and pleasure are sacred and worthy of reverence. In this spiritual framework, the focus shifts from sacrifice to embracing personal fulfillment, liberation, and the embodiment of the divine within oneself.

While some witches may offer small tokens of gratitude to certain spirits, it is essential to emphasize that such offerings are not sacrificial nor obligatory. Witchcraft recognizes that spirituality is a deeply personal journey, and practitioners can shape their practices based on their beliefs and experiences. The following excerpt from my version of the Charge remains true to the original sentiment.

> Listen close, my seekers of the light,
> For I am the Goddess, shining ever bright.
> No sacrifices needed, let that be known,
> In love's embrace, your power is grown.
> All acts of love and pleasure are my rites,
> In them, my children, find your soul's delights.
> Embrace your desires, let passion be your guide,
> For in your joy, my energy shall reside.
> Release the old ways, with compassion you'll find,
> All hearts connected, in a love that's kind.
> Walk your path, with honor and respect,
> In unity and love, our spirits intersect.
> Hold sacred all life, the web we weave,
> With gentle hands, let kindness achieve.
> In nature's cycles, see the reflection true,
> The ebb and flow, the wisdom that's imbued.

Monday 9

☽♐ 12:26 pm

Tuesday 10

World Suicide Prevention Day

Wednesday 11

☽ 1:05 am
☽v/c 3:06 am - ☽♑ 9:38 pm

Thursday 12

Friday 13

☽v/c 12:00 pm
Friday the 13th

Saturday 14

☽♒ 2:54 am

Sunday 15

☽v/c 2:08 pm

Autumn Equinox

The autumn equinox Sabbat is also known as Mabon. It is a time of balance and gratitude for the Earth's abundance and a time to prepare for the introspective months ahead. Here are a few ideas for your celebrations:

Apple Picking: Visit an orchard and partake in the tradition of apple picking, or pick up seasonal apples at your grocer or farmer's market. Use the apples in baking, or make home-made cider. Slice through an apple sideways to reveal its star. Say this charm and eat an apple slice to harness its protective powers.

Apple of protection, strong and true,
Shield me now in all I do.
Guard me with your magical might;
keep me safe both day and night.

Gratitude Ritual: Set up a sacred space or altar dedicated to gratitude. Meditate on the things you are thankful for and write them down. Place your notes on your altar and light a candle as an offering.

Shared Abundance: Decorate your dining table or altar with a cornucopia, gourds, and seasonal flowers and foliage. Gather your coven, friends, or loved ones. All participants form a circle and hold onto a rope, creating a physical and energetic connection. The circle represents unity and the shared intention of the group. Take turns expressing what you are grateful for. Gather the rope and place it on the dining table or altar when everyone has spoken and enjoy a meal together. Pot-luck meals embrace the theme of sharing, and may include seasonal fruits, vegetables, and grains.

Nature Scavenger Hunt: Organize a scavenger hunt in nature, focusing on items that represent the beauty of autumn. Participants can search for specific leaves, pinecones, or seeds. Encourage mindful observation and connection with the changing environment while respecting nature.

Monday 16

☽♓ 4:39 am

Tuesday 17

☽v/c 9:34 pm
○ 9:34 pm (Super)
Partial Lunar Eclipse

Wednesday 18

☽♈ 4:24 am

Thursday 19

☽v/c 10:13 pm

Friday 20

☽♉ 4:03 am

Saturday 21

Sunday 22

☀♎ 7:43 am
❀ Mabon 7:43 am
☽v/c 5:13 am - ☽♊ 5:25 am

Crafting Incense

Making incense is a creative and rewarding way to add fragrance and intention to your rituals. Here's a simple recipe to make loose incense:

Ingredients

- **2 tablespoons white sandalwood powder**
- **2 teaspoons resin**
  Choose from any one or a combination of resins based on your intentions, such as frankincense, myrrh, benzoin, or copal.
- **1 teaspoon dried herbs**
  Choose from any one or a combination of plants based on your intentions such as sage, rosemary, or lavender.
- **1 teaspoon powdered spices**
  Choose from any one or a combination of spices such as cinnamon, cloves, allspice, nutmeg, or star anise. Cinnamon is a good all-purpose choice.
- **Optional: 6-12 drops of Essential Oils**
  Use the guide on page 32 and choose an oil based on your intentions and its flashpoint.

Directions

- Grind the dried herbs, spices, and essential oils (if selected) using a mortar and pestle. Add the resins and crush until you achieve a coarse powder. As you blend the ingredients, infuse them with your intentions and the purpose you want the incense to serve.

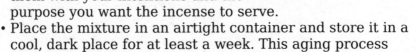

Star Anise

Cinnamon

Cloves

- Place the mixture in an airtight container and store it in a cool, dark place for at least a week. This aging process allows the scents to meld and deepen.
- Place a small pile of incense on a heat-resistant dish or charcoal burner. Light the edge of the mixture and let it smolder, releasing its aromatic smoke. If your incense doesn't burn well with this method, use an incense charcoal in a cauldron filled with sand. Ignite the charcoal, and add a pinch of your incense to it.

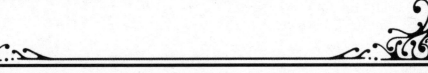

Monday 23

International Celebrate Bisexuality Day

Tuesday 24

◑ 1:49 pm
☽v/c 3:13 am - ☽♋ 9:50 am

Wednesday 25

☽v/c 12:51 pm

Thursday 26

☽♌ 5:48 pm

Friday 27

Saturday 28

☽v/c 11:04 am

Sunday 29

☽♍ 4:42 am

October

Mon	Tue	Wed	Thr	Fri	Sat	Sun
	1	2 ●	3	4	5	6
7	8	9	10 ◑	11	12	13
14	15	16	17 ○	18	19	20
21	22	23	24 ◐	25	26	27
28	29	30	31 ✺			

- Breast Cancer Awareness Month
- LGBTQIA+ History Month
- National Apple Month
- Bat Appreciation Month

Notes

_____

_____

_____

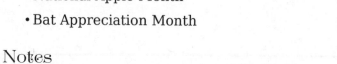

1	
2	
3	
4	
5	
6	
7	
8	
9	
10	
11	
12	
13	
14	
15	
16	
17	
18	
19	
20	
21	
22	
23	
24	
25	
26	
27	
28	
29	
30	
31	

Tarot Cards vs. Oracle Cards

Tarot cards and oracle cards are widely used as tools for divination and spiritual guidance, but they possess distinct characteristics. Tarot cards are an ancient system of 78 cards divided into Major Arcana and Minor Arcana, each with its own symbolism and meaning. They follow a structured system, offering rich imagery and complex interpretations that delve into the human experience and archetypal energies.

On the other hand, oracle cards are a more modern invention and come in various deck sizes and themes. Unlike tarot, oracle cards lack a standardized structure and can vary significantly in content and design. They often focus on specific themes, such as fairies, animals, or affirmations, and provide intuitive guidance and insights into various aspects of life.

While tarot cards usually rely on predetermined meanings and traditional interpretations, oracle cards offer more flexibility and personal interpretation. Although some tarot readers use their cards without considering the traditional definitions, this is not a common practice except for personal single-card draws. Both tarot and oracle cards can be powerful tools for self-reflection, divination, and spiritual growth. The choice between them depends on your personal preference.

Chipotle Apple Butter BBQ Sauce

Ingredients

- 7 oz can of Chipotle Peppers in Adobo Sauce
- 16-32 oz (2-4 cups) Apple Butter (recipe on page 160)
- 2 teaspoons Onion Powder
- Optional: 3-10 drops Liquid Smoke Flavoring

Directions

- Blend chipotle peppers and adobo sauce until smooth and set aside. Add the apple butter to the empty (but unwashed) blender along with the onion powder and a third to a half of the pureed peppers. Use more if you like your food spicy!
- Taste your mixture for the level of heat and add more chipotle as desired. Add more onion powder to suit your tastes and season with liquid smoke for extra smokiness.

Monday 30

☽v/c 11:29 pm

Tuesday 1

☽♎ 5:20 pm
World Vegetarian Day

Wednesday 2

● 1:49 pm (Micro)

Thursday 3

☽v/c 12:40 pm

Friday 4

☽♏ 6:23 am

Saturday 5

☽v/c 5:26 pm

Sunday 6

☽♐ 6:34 pm

Layouts for Cleromancy

Divination spreads, or layouts, are used with tarot cards, oracle cards, runes, dice, and other forms of divination in which you cast lots (cleromancy). Spreads are a way in which you arrange or layout your divination tools to give you a better understanding of their meaning to you. Before you begin a divination session, decide which layout you will use and what the positions will mean.

Below is a simple yet powerful layout that will help provide clarity and illumination. Focus on your question and draw your lots for each position from one to seven.

1. **You**
   This position represents you.
2. **What is Hidden**
   This position reveals what is hidden from you, either by yourself or others.
3. **Mitigation**
   This represents influences that will change or alter the probable outcome.
4. **Blocks**
   This reveals what stands in your way of success.
5. **Past**
   Reveals the influences that led to the current situation.
6. **Present**
   Represents the current situation.
7. **Future**
   This is the most likely outcome if things continue as they have without the influence of position 3. If your result is not what you want, look to the third position for clues to change the probabilities.

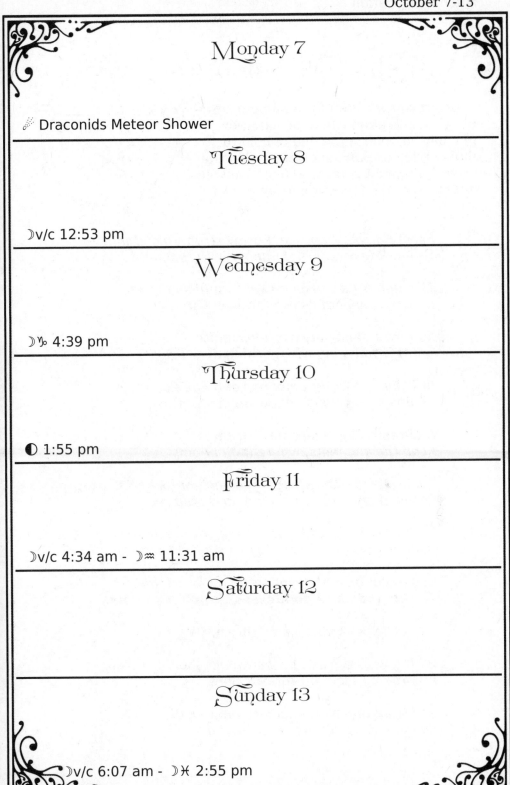

Monday 7

Draconids Meteor Shower

Tuesday 8

☽v/c 12:53 pm

Wednesday 9

☽♑ 4:39 pm

Thursday 10

☽ 1:55 pm

Friday 11

☽v/c 4:34 am - ☽♒ 11:31 am

Saturday 12

Sunday 13

☽v/c 6:07 am - ☽♓ 2:55 pm

Witch's Invocation

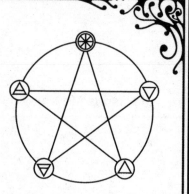

Use this invocation for a naming ceremony, a dedication ritual, or initiation.
You may customize the line in bold to
align with your path, such as "To Hecate,
I give my name." After that line, you will
state your legal name or chosen name.

From Earth's embrace, I draw strength and might,
Grounding my spirit, aligning with the night.

Through Air's whispers, wisdom fills my mind,
Guiding my path as mysteries unwind.

By Fire's flame, my passions ignite,
Transforming my will, burning ever bright.

In Water's depths, emotions ebb and flow,
Cleansing my spirit, allowing me to grow.

Embracing my magic deep within,
I call the elements, where it all begins.

Grant me the knowledge, the ancient lore,
To wield my craft, to explore and restore.

With reverence and love, I seek your embrace,
Ancient ones, guide me in this sacred space.

In dedication and devotion, I now proclaim,
To the gods and goddesses, I give my name.

* Speak your name thrice. *

With love and trust, my spirit will soar,
Embracing the craft forevermore.

As I walk this path under moonlit skies,
So mote it be, let my magic arise!

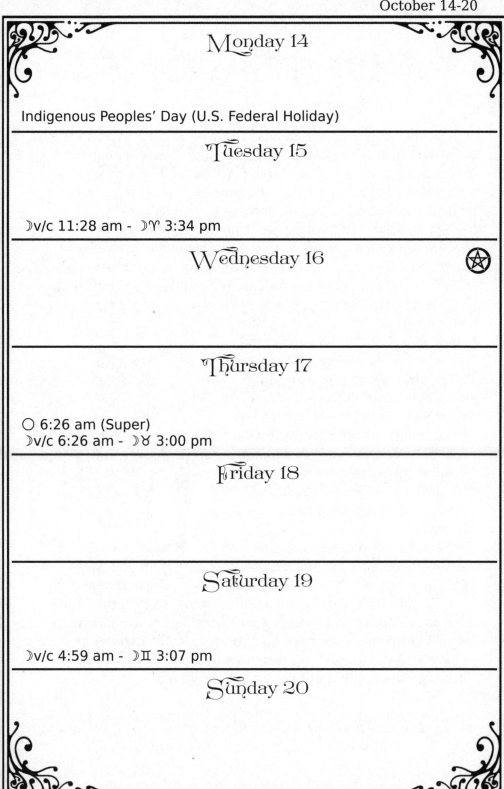

Monday 14

Indigenous Peoples' Day (U.S. Federal Holiday)

Tuesday 15

☽v/c 11:28 am - ☽♈ 3:34 pm

Wednesday 16 ⊛

Thursday 17

○ 6:26 am (Super)
☽v/c 6:26 am - ☽♉ 3:00 pm

Friday 18

Saturday 19

☽v/c 4:59 am - ☽♊ 3:07 pm

Sunday 20

Wax On — Wax Off
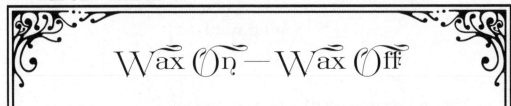

Witches burn a lot of candles, and with that lifestyle comes a bit of practical housekeeping. No amount of wax spillage will deter us from enjoying our candle rituals, and wax dripped over your candle holder can be enchanting. But, wax spills on your favorite altar cloth or ritual robe can cause distress.

Not to worry! Removing wax from fabric and carpets can be daunting but manageable with the proper techniques. Toss small items like altar cloths and tarot bags in the freezer. Once the wax is frozen, scrape it off using the edge of a credit card.

Large items like carpets can be treated with ice packs or ice cubes in a plastic bag. Let the ice harden the wax, then scrape off what you can.

After the freezing and scraping step, cover the spill with two or three paper towels. Apply a warm iron to melt the wax, which the towel will absorb. Be cautious not to damage fabric or carpet with excessive heat.

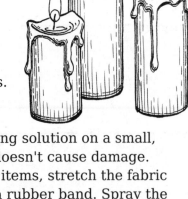

Colored candles, especially red, purple, and black, tend to leave stains. Blot any remaining residue with a cloth soaked in rubbing alcohol or carpet cleaner. Always test any cleaning solution on a small, inconspicuous area first to ensure it doesn't cause damage.

If you still have residue on smaller items, stretch the fabric across a colander and secure it with a rubber band. Spray the stained area with a degreaser or rub with dish soap and pour boiling water through the fabric where the stain remains. Repeat as necessary until the stain disappears.

Trivia: The tallest candle ever recorded stood almost 80 feet tall and was lit in Stockholm, Sweden in 2011.

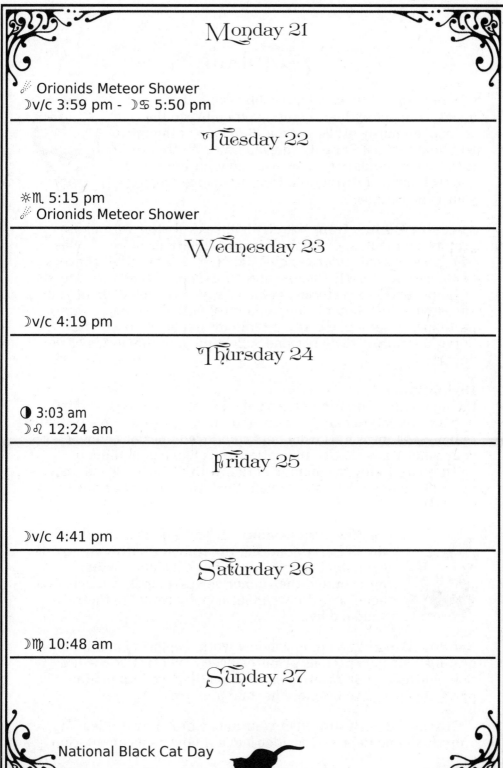

Monday 21

☄ Orionids Meteor Shower
☽v/c 3:59 pm - ☽♋ 5:50 pm

Tuesday 22

☀♏ 5:15 pm
☄ Orionids Meteor Shower

Wednesday 23

☽v/c 4:19 pm

Thursday 24

☽ 3:03 am
☽♌ 12:24 am

Friday 25

☽v/c 4:41 pm

Saturday 26

☽♍ 10:48 am

Sunday 27

National Black Cat Day

Samhain

Samhain is a time to honor the cycles of life and death, connect with ancestors, and embrace the reflective energy of the season. Samhain is the third and final harvest Sabbat. The veil between the worlds is thin now, making it a powerful time for ancestral connections and divination. Here are some ideas for your celebrations:

Ancestor Connection: Set up an ancestral altar with photographs, mementos, or symbolic representations of loved ones who have passed. Offer candles, flowers, and heartfelt prayers to connect with their wisdom and guidance. Gather with friends or family and share stories, memories, or anecdotes about your ancestors. Host a dumb supper, a meal eaten in silence, where participants set a place at the table for departed loved ones. Serve their favorite dishes and reflect on your memories of the departed.

Divination:
Engage in divination practices such as tarot readings, scrying, or rune casting to gain insights and guidance from the spiritual realm. Seek messages from departed loved ones or connect with your inner wisdom. Use divination tools like a pendulum or spirit board to invite communication with departed loved ones or spirit guides. Always approach this practice with reverence and caution.

Masked Procession: Organize a masked procession or party honoring the transformative energy of Samhain. Participants might consider costumes representing their inner selves, spirits, or aspects of themselves they cannot usually reveal in their mundane lives.

Shadow Work: Engage in shadow work, exploring and integrating your unconscious or unresolved aspects. Use meditation, journaling, or creative expression to delve into hidden parts of yourself to promote healing and growth.

Graveyard Tending: Visit your ancestors' graves, cleaning up trash and debris. Consider leaving flowers as an offering.

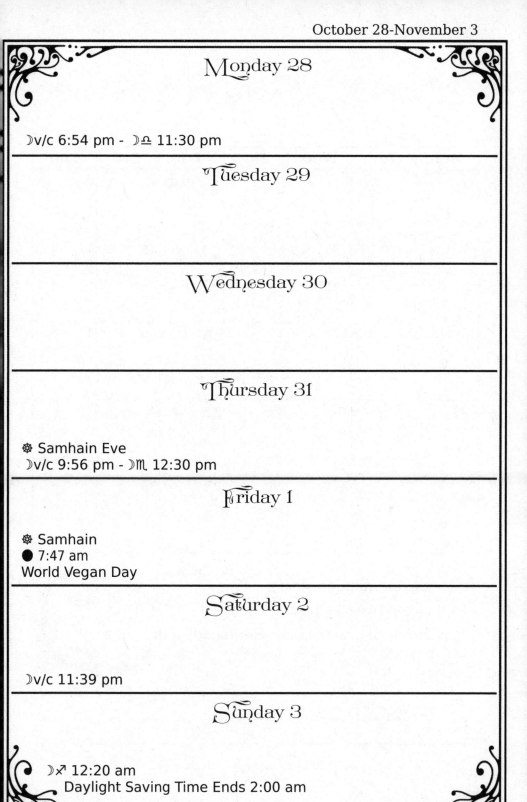

Monday 28

☽v/c 6:54 pm - ☽♎ 11:30 pm

Tuesday 29

Wednesday 30

Thursday 31

❀ Samhain Eve
☽v/c 9:56 pm - ☽♏ 12:30 pm

Friday 1

❀ Samhain
● 7:47 am
World Vegan Day

Saturday 2

☽v/c 11:39 pm

Sunday 3

☽♐ 12:20 am
Daylight Saving Time Ends 2:00 am

November

Mon	Tue	Wed	Thr	Fri	Sat	Sun
				1 ❋●	2	3
4	5	6 ⊗	7	8 ◐	9	10
11	12	13	14	15 ○	16	17
18	19	20	21	22 ◐	23	24
25 ☿℞	26	27	28	29	30	

- National Gratitude Month
- National Diabetes Month
- National Native American Heritage Month

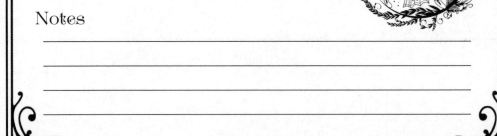

Notes

_____

_____

_____

_____

1	●	
2	●	
3	●	
4	●	
5	●	
6	◑	
7	◑	
8	◑	
9	◑	
10	◑	
11	◔	
12	○	
13	○	
14	○	
15	○	
16	○	
17	○	
18	○	
19	◗	
20	◗	
21	◐	
22	◐	
23	◐	
24	◑	
25	◖	
26	◖	
27	◖	
28	●	
29	●	
30	●	

Profanity, Cursing & Curses

Curses, curse words, and profanity have long held a fascinating and controversial place in human language and culture. Beyond their emotional impact, these linguistic expressions carry a rich tapestry of psychological and physiological aspects.

Curses, in the context of supernatural or magical beliefs, are believed to possess the power to bring harm or misfortune upon individuals. This belief has its roots in various cultures and folklore traditions worldwide, where curses are seen as potent tools for invoking negative energies or divine retribution.

On the other hand, curse words and profanity tap into the depths of human emotion, serving as a release valve for frustration, anger, or shock. Psychologically, they can offer a sense of catharsis, allowing individuals to vent their feelings and relieve tension.

Physiologically, the act of swearing has been found to trigger a stress response in the body, leading to the release of adrenaline and increased heart rate. Studies suggest that uttering curse words can provide a temporary pain-relieving effect by activating the body's natural analgesic response.

While curses and curse words can evoke strong reactions, their impact varies significantly across cultures and individuals. Social norms, personal values, and context are crucial in determining the acceptability and consequences of using such language.

You can use profanity in spells to help you release energy. For this to work, you must experiment with your selection of words, finding the most potent personal triggers for release.

As language evolves, the complex interplay between curses, curse words, and profanity remains fascinating. Whether viewed through the lens of magic, emotional release, or physiological responses, these linguistic expressions continue to shape our understanding of human communication and the intricate nuances of expression.

Banishing & Bond Breaking Example Invocation

With every breath, I exhale your presence,
No longer shall you linger, causing grievance.
Begone, negativity! Get the f*** out,
Vanish now and forever, without a doubt.

Monday 4

☽v/c 5:50 pm
☄ Taurids Meteor Shower

Tuesday 5

☽♑ 9:18 am
U.S. General Election Day
☄ Taurids Meteor Shower

Wednesday 6

⊗ 4:10 pm
☽v/c 1:11 pm

Thursday 7

☽♒ 4:58 pm

Friday 8

◑ 11:55 pm

Saturday 9

☽v/c 6:23 pm - ☽♓ 10:00 pm

Sunday 10

Non-Binary Witchcraft

There is an ever-growing embrace of inclusivity, diversity, and personal exploration in witchcraft. Non-binary witchcraft is a path that honors and celebrates the fluidity of gender identities, transcending traditional notions of male and female. It offers a space where practitioners can connect with the spiritual realm in a way that resonates with their unique identities.

One aspect of non-binary witchcraft is reimagining our perceptions of Goddesses and Gods. Rather than adhering strictly to the gender binary, non-binary witches often honor and work with deities that embody a spectrum of gender expressions. We recognize that the divine is not limited to masculine or feminine energies alone. Instead, we seek balance by embracing a diverse pantheon.

Non-binary witchcraft invites you to forge personal connections with deities that resonate with your unique understanding of gender and spirituality. It encourages you to explore and discover your sacred truths, creating a space to experience the divine beyond societal constraints.

As non-binary witchcraft evolves, it fosters a more inclusive and expansive understanding of the spiritual realm. By embracing the fluidity of gender identities and reimagining the divine, we embark on a transformative journey that celebrates the beauty of diversity and affirms the power of personal connection in magical practices.

I've noted below a few deities that may interest you. The interpretation and understanding of these entities may vary among practitioners and cultural contexts.

Aphroditus — A blending of the Greek deities Aphrodite and Hermes, embodying feminine and masculine qualities.
The Morrigan — A Celtic goddess known to shift between different forms and genders.
Hapi — An ancient Egyptian deity of the Nile River, embodying the nurturing and life-giving aspects of both masculine and feminine energies.
Lempo — A Finnish deity described as non-binary or gender-fluid.
Metis — In Greek mythology, Metis is associated with masculine and feminine qualities.

Monday 11

Einherjar
☽v/c 7:16 am
Veterans Day (U.S. Federal Holiday)

Tuesday 12

☽♈ 12:26 am

Wednesday 13

☽v/c 7:50 am

Thursday 14

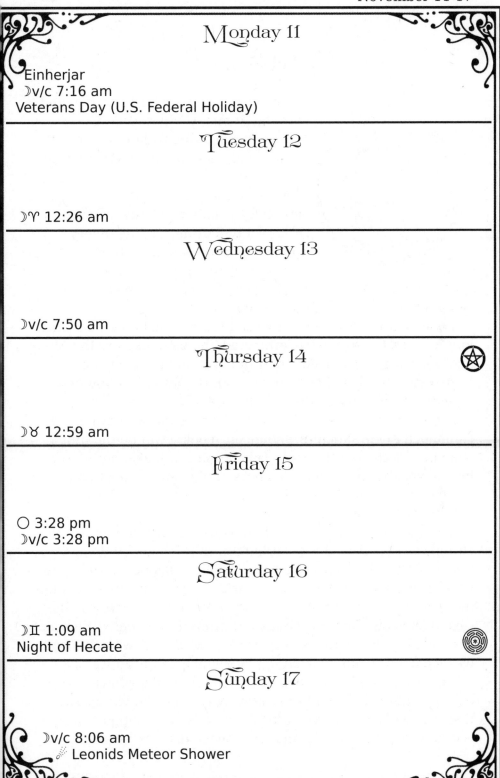

☽♉ 12:59 am

Friday 15

○ 3:28 pm
☽v/c 3:28 pm

Saturday 16

☽♊ 1:09 am
Night of Hecate

Sunday 17

☽v/c 8:06 am
Leonids Meteor Shower

Artemis II

Artemis is a Greek Goddess equated with the Roman Goddess Diana[6]. Artemis has a twin brother, Apollo. While Apollo is a Sun deity, Artemis is a lunar deity.

NASA's Apollo missions in the 1960s and 1970s consisted of nine missions with twenty-four astronauts. Every Apollo astronaut was a white male.

Twelve walked on the Moon while six drove roving vehicles, and the remaining stayed in orbit. No woman has ever been to the Moon.

In November 2022 we witnessed the Artemis I mission. This mission was the first of several, enabling us to explore the Moon and Mars while inspiring a new generation of exploration.

Artemis II is scheduled for this month and will be the first crewed mission to the Moon in decades. This mission will include the first female astronaut on the Moon (Christina Hammock Koch). Koch (pronounced "cook") will be the first woman to walk on the Moon. This mission will also herald the first lunar mission including a person of color (Victor Glover). Reid Wiseman and Jeremy Hansen will accompany Koch and Glover for this ten-day mission.

The spacecraft we're launching is named Orion. Like Artemis, Orion was considered a great hunter. In the book by Robert Graves entitled *The Greek Myths*, Apollo is jealous of the deep friendship between Artemis and Orion. While Orion was swimming in the ocean, Apollo challenged Artemis's archery skills, saying she could not hit the distant figure in the water. She shot and killed Orion. Artemis was stricken with grief when his body washed ashore and decided to place him among the stars.

The Artemis missions will establish the Artemis Base Camp on the surface and build the Gateway to orbit the Moon. The Gateway will serve as an outpost with essential support for exploration of the Moon and deep space explorations.

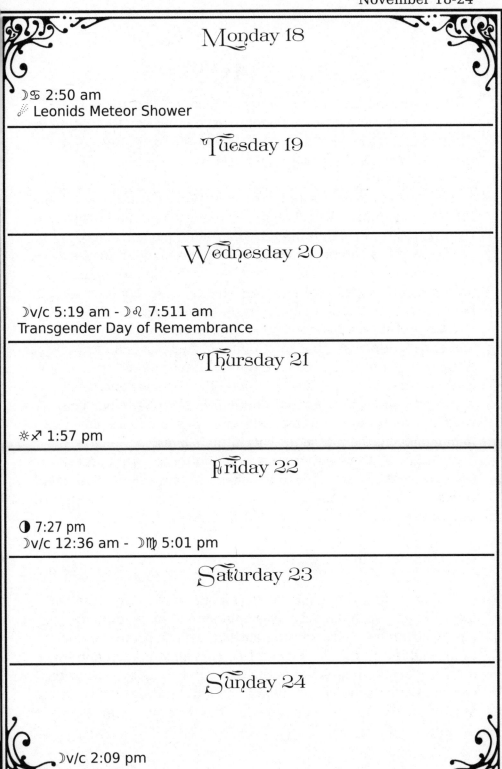

Monday 18

☽♋ 2:50 am
Leonids Meteor Shower

Tuesday 19

Wednesday 20

☽v/c 5:19 am - ☽♌ 7:511 am
Transgender Day of Remembrance

Thursday 21

⚹♐ 1:57 pm

Friday 22

☽ 7:27 pm
☽v/c 12:36 am - ☽♍ 5:01 pm

Saturday 23

Sunday 24

☽v/c 2:09 pm

Tea Leaf Reading

Tea leaf reading, or tasseography, is an ancient divination practice that has captivated people for centuries. Originating in China and later spreading to the Middle East and Europe, it involves interpreting patterns formed by tea leaves at the bottom of a cup.

The process begins with the preparation of a cup of loose-leaf tea. I prefer gunpowder-style green tea or a long-leaf oolong for readings. After drinking the tea, the remaining leaves are swirled around and poured out, leaving a residue of leaves at the bottom of the cup. The reader then carefully examines the patterns, shapes, and symbols left behind. Each configuration is believed to hold hidden meanings and messages.

Interpreting tea leaves requires a combination of intuition and knowledge of symbolism. Common shapes, such as circles, triangles, or lines, can indicate different aspects of life, such as love, fortune, or travel. The position of the shapes and their relation to each other further add depth to the reading. The reader's experience and understanding of symbolism play a part in deciphering the messages within the leaves.

Whether approached as entertainment or spiritual practice, tea leaf reading continues to fascinate and intrigue individuals seeking a deeper connection to themselves and the mysteries of the universe.

Further Studies

The next time you make yourself a cup of tea, use loose-leaf tea without a strainer. When the remaining tea in your cup barely covers the leaves at the bottom, swirl it around a few times and tip it onto the saucer. Use your imagination and intuition to discern shapes left in the tea. You can look up what the various symbols mean online, but you'll get more out of your tea session when you contemplate what the different symbols mean to you.

Monday 25

☿℞
)♎ 5:20 am

Tuesday 26

Wednesday 27

)v/c 3:14 am -)♏ 5:21 pm

Thursday 28

Thanksgiving Day (U.S. Federal Holiday)

Friday 29

)v/c 12:50 pm

Saturday 30

)♐ 5:53 am

Sunday 1

● 12:21 am
)v/c 7:28 pm

December

Mon	Tue	Wed	Thr	Fri	Sat	Sun
						1 ●
2	3	4	5	6	7	8 ◑
9	10	11	12	13	14	15 ○ ☿R Ends
16	17	18	19	20	21 ❈	22 ◑
23	24	25	26	27	28	29
30 ●	31					

- Human Rights Month
- Spiritual Literacy Month

Notes

_____

_____

1	
2	
3	
4	
5	
6	
7	
8	
9	
10	
11	
12	
13	
14	
15	
16	
17	
18	
19	
20	
21	
22	
23	
24	
25	
26	
27	
28	
29	
30	
31	

Tipping Guide for Witches

Tipping is customary to show appreciation for good service, and is expected in the United States. Although tipping is a personal choice, many employers create work environments where tips are relied upon by staff to survive.

Ultimately, tipping is a gesture of gratitude and appreciation. When calculating a tip, consider local customs and any service charges that may already be included with the bill. Most of us are aware that you leave a 15-20% tip at restaurants. This guide is for the less familiar service industries where tipping is appropriate.

1. Psychic Readers: 15-20% is the standard tip for a tarot reading or other psychic services. Most readers work as independent contractors and pay a percentage of their fees to the establishment where they are set up.

2. Bartenders: A common guideline is to tip bartenders 15-20% of the total drink bill or $1-2 per drink, depending on the complexity and quality of the service.

3. Hotel Services: For hotel staff, such as bellhops, concierge, or housekeeping, it is customary to tip $1-2 per bag, $5-10 for concierge services, and $2-5 per night for housekeeping.

4. Henna Designs: Like most personal services such as hairstylists or spa treatments, a tip of 15%-20% of the total cost is appreciated.

5. Taxis, Lyft, Uber, and other Ride Services: 15-20%, and for fares under $10 it is a good idea to tip a flat $5.

6. Officiants: For handfasting, Wiccanings, and other rituals involving clergy or a hired officiant, it is customary to tip 15-25% with a minimum of $20.

7. Energy Services: Tip for reiki, house cleansing rituals, and other energy services at 15-20%.

Monday 2

Tuesday 3

☽ ♑ 3:09 pm
Rites of Bona Dea

Wednesday 4

☽v/c 5:33 pm - ☽ ♒ 10:21 pm

Thursday 5

Friday 6

☽v/c 3:52

Saturday 7

☽ ♓ 3:49 am

Sunday 8

☽ 9:26 am
☽v/c 9:26 am

Names of the Moons

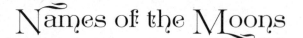

There are many different names for the same full moon in any given month or season. This variety is entirely appropriate, as regional and cultural differences are reflected in the names.

This list contains the historical moon names with the most common name for a month's moon is listed first. You can create your own names for the moons based on your experiences, observations, and preferences.

January	Wolf Moon*, Nursing Moon, Winter Moon, Milk Moon, Cold Moon
February	Storm or Snow Moon, Horning Moon, Fasting or Hunger Moon, Weaning Moon
March	Worm Moon, Seed Moon, Chaste Moon, Planter's Moon, Sap Moon
April	Hare Moon, Mating Moon, Frog Moon, Flower Moon, Seed Moon, Egg Moon
May	Dyad Moon, Journey Moon, Mead Moon, Strawberry Moon, Rose Moon, Milk Moon
June	Honey or Mead Moon, Strawberry Moon, Hay Moon, Wort Moon, Mother's Moon
July	Wort Moon, Hay Moon, Grain Moon, Father's Moon, Barley Moon, Elk Moon
August	Barley Moon, Nesting Moon, Harvest Moon, Wine Moon, Sturgeon Moon
September	Harvest Moon, Wine Moon, Barley Moon
October	Blood Moon, Harvest Moon, Hunting Moon, Culling Moon, Pumpkin Moon
November	Snow Moon, Beaver Moon, Death Moon, Oak Moon
December	Cold Moon, Big Moon, Oak Moon, Long Night's Moon, Wolf Moon*

* The Wolf Moon is the first Full Moon after the December Solstice.

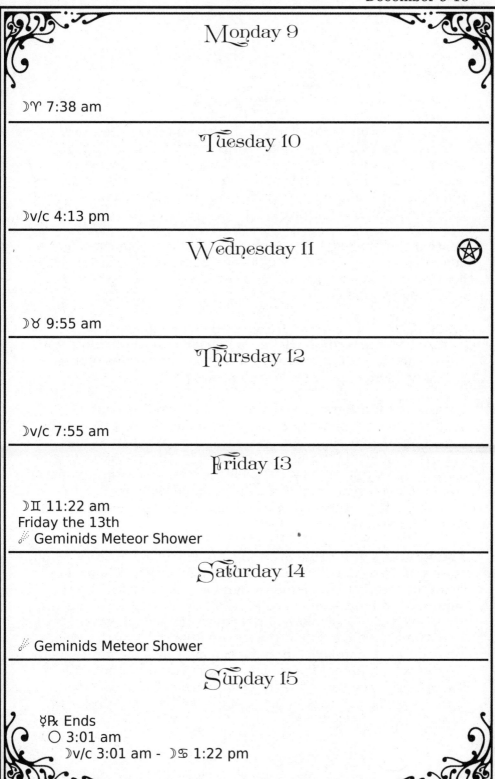

Monday 9

☽♈ 7:38 am

Tuesday 10

☽v/c 4:13 pm

Wednesday 11 ⊛

☽♉ 9:55 am

Thursday 12

☽v/c 7:55 am

Friday 13

☽♊ 11:22 am
Friday the 13th
Geminids Meteor Shower

Saturday 14

Geminids Meteor Shower

Sunday 15

☿℞ Ends
○ 3:01 am
☽v/c 3:01 am - ☽♋ 1:22 pm

Yule

The days grow increasingly short leading up to the winter solstice. The Yule Sabbat honors the sun's return and light's rebirth. It is a time of hope and renewal in the dark days of winter. Embrace the magic and wonder of the winter solstice as you create meaningful Yule traditions. Adapt these ideas to suit your beliefs and preferences.

Festive Decor: Yule trees, wreaths, Yule logs, pinecones, holly, mistletoe, and evergreen boughs are traditional decor for the home and altar. Evergreen foliage symbolizes life's persistent nature during the darkest times.

Spice it Up: Cinnamon, cloves, nutmeg, and ginger are warming spices traditionally used in baking during the winter. These spices also contribute their magical properties of prosperity, attraction, protection, and healing.

Candle Ritual: Right before the exact time of the winter solstice, shut off all the lights in your home. In the darkness, reflect on the blessings and lessons of the past year. At the precise solstice, light a white candle and visualize light growing within you as you set intentions for the winter season. You may continue to burn additional candles around the home, welcoming the returning light and greeting the new solar year with hope and optimism.

The Winter's Tale: Yule brings us a special type of storytelling, often reflecting darkness and madness, followed by hope and renewal. Whether you gather around a cozy fire with others or enjoy a good book alone in candlelight, winter tales can inspire creativity and help explore our shadows. Like Shakespeare's *The Winter's Tale*, Yuletide stories are often filled with psychological drama, happily ending in comedy. These themes reflect the darkness waning, the returning light within us, and the literal world. You can make up your own stories or consider some movies and books. A list of suggested winter tales is on page 152.

Monday 16

☽v/c 12:33 pm

Tuesday 17

☽♌ 5:39 pm
Saturnalia Begins

Wednesday 18

Thursday 19

☽v/c 11:19 pm

Friday 20

☽♍ 1:37 am

Saturday 21

☼♑ 3:20 am
☽v/c 5:54 am
❀ Yule 3:20 am
☄ Ursids Meteor Shower

Sunday 22

☽ 4:18 pm
☽♎ 1:08 pm
☄ Ursids Meteor Shower

 Ritual Bells

   Rituals utilize bells to cleanse spaces, summon spirits, ward off negativity, and honor sacred moments. Ancient cultures recognized the power of sound; wisdom reflected in the modern practice of sound baths. Drawing inspiration from these age-old beliefs, sound baths employ bells and other musical instruments to create therapeutic resonances, facilitating relaxation and healing. Singing bowls create a meditative ambiance and foster inner harmony. These instruments serve as conduits, heightening spiritual experiences and connecting you to mystical forces within and beyond. Communities worldwide engage in collective bell ringing around the winter holidays, transcending cultural boundaries and fostering unity. Here are four ways you can use bells in your rituals:

Casting and Clearing: The sound of the bell is used to mark the boundaries when casting a circle, creating a protective barrier. The bell's ringing also helps clear the space of any negative or stagnant energy, purifying the area for the ritual work.

Invocation and Communication: Use bells to invoke and communicate with spirits, deities, or otherworldly entities. The clear tones of the bell can serve as a signal or call to these energies, inviting their presence and participation in the ritual. You can also use bells to establish a connection between the witch and the spiritual realm, facilitating communication or receiving messages.

Focus and Intent: Sound helps you focus your energy and intention during spellcasting or ritual work. As the bell rings, the vibrations generated can amplify the witch's intent and direct their energy towards the desired outcome. Ring your ritual bell at the end of a spell to send the energy forth for manifestation.

Transitions and Ritual Phases: Bells are rung to mark different phases or transitions within a ritual, such as the beginning or conclusion of specific actions or the initiation of a new stage. The ringing can signify a shift in energy, the completion of one aspect of the ritual, or the opening of a gateway to a different realm.

Monday 23

Saturnalia Ends

Tuesday 24

☽v/c 4:43 am

Wednesday 25

☽♏ 2:07 am
Christmas Day (U.S. Federal Holiday)

Thursday 26

☽v/c 11:07 pm

Friday 27

☽♐ 1:47 pm

Saturday 28

Sunday 29

☽v/c 2:02 pm - ☽♑ 10:38 pm

Bottle & Bag Charms

Making a charm is a great way to focus your intentions. Use these instructions to create either a spell bottle or a spell bag. You will need a small glass or plastic container with a tight-fitting lid to make a spell bottle. A spell bag is a small pouch that fits easily in your hand. It can be made of leather or fabric, and you can choose a color that corresponds to your intentions.

The correspondences section of your almanac will help you select the ingredients you need. Your charm is a personal tool, so trust your intuition when selecting herbs and stones. Experiment with different combinations and techniques to find what resonates best with you.

- Select three or more herbs that align with your intention or desired outcome.
- Choose one or more stones or crystals that complements your intention.
- Pass your spell bag through incense smoke while visualizing any stagnant or negative energies being released and purified. If you use a spell bottle, tip it over burning incense to fill it with cleansing smoke.
- Fill your pouch or bottle with the chosen herbs and stones. As you add each ingredient, focus on your intention and visualize your desired outcome. You can speak a simple incantation or affirmation as you work.
- Close or tie the bag, or seal the bottle tightly. You may seal your bottle with wax in a color that corresponds to your intent.
- Hold your bag or bottle and infuse it with energy and intention. Visualize it radiating with the infused power.

Monday 30

● 4:26 pm (Black Moon)
Good time for banishing.

Tuesday 31

☽v/c 1:02 am
New Year's Eve

Wednesday, January 1, 2023

☽≈ 4:50 am
New Year's Day

Thursday 2

☽v/c 8:33 pm

Friday 3

☽✶ 9:21 am

Saturday 4

Sunday 5

☽v/c 5:57 am - ☽♈ 1:01 m

Apogee & Perigee

Apogee (ăp′ə-jē) is the point in the Moon's orbit when it is farthest away from Earth. Perigee (pĕr′ə-jē) is the point in its orbit when it is closest to Earth. The moon is nearly 31,000 miles closer to us at perigee.

The Moon's distance from us affects the tides, winds, climate, and weather patterns. It may also affect your energy, moods, and magic. You can use the following worksheets to note your energy levels for apogee and perigee. These times and dates are also noted in the Lunar Planner Pages and the Weekly Planner Pages.

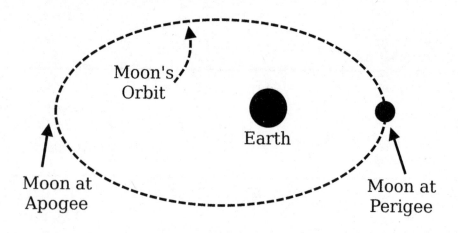

Apogee

Date	Time	Mood & Magic
Jan 1	9:28 am	
Jan 29	2:14 am	
Feb 25	8:59 am	
Mar 23	10:45 am	
Apr 19	9:10 pm	
May 17	1:58 pm	

Apogee

Jun 14	8:35 am	
Jul 12	3:11 am	
Aug 8	8:31 pm	
Sep 5	9:53 am	
Oct 2	**2:39 pm**	
Oct 29	5:50 pm	
Nov 26	5:55 am	
Dec 24	1:24 am	

The farthest distance of the Moon to the Earth this year is October 2nd.

Perigee

Date	Time	Mood & Magic
Jan 13	4:34 am	
Feb 10	12:52 pm	
Mar 10	**1:04 am**	
Apr 7	12:50 pm	
May 5	5:04 pm	
Jun 2	2:16 am	
Jun 27	6:30 am	
Jul 24	12:41 am	
Aug 21	12:02 am	
Sep 18	8:23 am	
Oct 16	7:51 pm	
Nov 14	5:14 am	
Dec 12	7:20 am	

March 10th marks the Moon's closest approach to Earth this year.

Perihelion and Aphelion

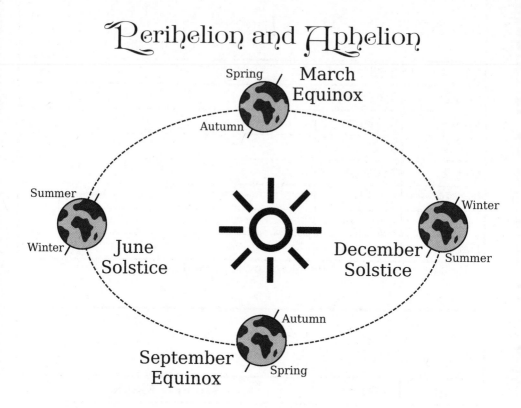

Perihelion occurs when the Earth is closest to the Sun. This happens a couple of weeks after the December solstice. In the northern hemisphere, it may seem counter-intuitive that the Sun is closer to us in winter than in summer. The reason for the seasons has more to do with the angle of the Earth than its distance from the Sun.

Imagine a line (axis) extending from the North Pole to the South Pole. This axis is angled about 22.1 to 24.5 degrees away from the Sun. The hemisphere angled toward the Sun is warmer. Even in December when the Sun is over three million miles closer to Earth, the axial tilt causes warmer weather in the southern hemisphere.

Aphelion is when Earth is farthest from the Sun. This happens a couple of weeks after the June solstice. At this time, the axis is angled toward the Sun causing warmer weather in the northern hemisphere.

2024 Perihelion - January 2, 2024 6:38 pm

2024 Aphelion - July 5, 2024 12:06 am

Eclipses

Total Solar Eclipse April 8

This is an exciting year for eclipses. The Great American Eclipse of 2024 is a highly anticipated total solar eclipse that will sweep across the United States on April 8th. Millions are set to gather along the path of totality, which will span across many populated areas of the world[7]. The Moon's passage in front of the Sun promises to create a captivating display, with darkness, a visible corona, and a drop in temperature.

This rare phenomenon will bring together astronomers, witches, scientists, and enthusiasts, attracting global tourists and fostering a shared appreciation for our solar system. The event will last under fourteen minutes in most locations, but will leave an unforgettable impression as a remarkable celestial spectacle and a unifying human experience.

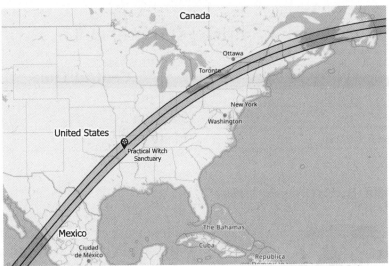

The path of totality for the eclipse on April 8, 2024.
Viewing is optimal in the banded area.

Eclipse Stages	Central Time
Moon's shadow hits Earth	10:42 am
Maximum Eclipse	1:17 pm
Moon's shadow passes Earth	3:52 pm

Annular Solar Eclipse October 2

This eclipse will only be visible in the southern areas of Africa. Even when an eclipse is not visible, we can work with the magical energies of the waxing and waning light and the alignment of the celestial bodies.

Penumbral Lunar Eclipse March 24-25

Eclipse Stages	Central Time
Eclipse Begins	Mar 24 at 11:53 pm
Peak	Mar 25 at 2:13 am
Eclipse Ends	Mar 25 at 4:32 am

Partial Lunar Eclipse September 17

Eclipse Stages	Central Time
Eclipse Begins	7:41 pm
Peak	9:44 pm
Eclipse Ends	11:47 pm

Lunar Eclipse Notes

Lunar eclipses occur during the full Moon, and the Moon cycles through the waning, new, and waxing phases during an eclipse. The unification of Earth and Moon energies can be felt as the Earth's shadow falls over the Moon. You can design your eclipse spells and rituals to harness these unique energies.

Working With Moon Phases

There are many approaches to working with the phases of the moon. This four-phase approach is easy to remember and flows naturally with the primary energies of the phases. If your technique is different than this, don't worry! You can use any approach that you feel is right for you.

New: Start new projects and spells for growth, manifestation, or new beginnings. This is also a good time for cleansing, clearing, and protection.

Keywords: Resting, releasing, banishing, repelling, reversal magic, unbinding, new beginnings.
When: New moon energy lasts for three days—the day before the new moon, the day of, and the day after.

Waxing: This phase is excellent for attraction, drawing, growth, and spells to bring what you desire into your life. Your intentions grow and manifest as the moon waxes.

Keywords: Attraction, setting intentions, manifesting, planning, planting, developing, drawing, attraction.
When: From two days after the new moon to two days before the full moon.

Full: This is a great time for any type of magic or divination, and is a time of celebration and gratitude.

Keywords: Celebration, harvest, gratitude, meditation, devotion, protection, magical power.
When: Full moon energy lasts for three days—the day before the full moon, the day of, and the day after.

Waning: This is a time of cleansing and releasing intentions that were not meant to manifest. Work on spells for reducing and banishing.

Keywords: Clearing, cleansing, releasing, reversals, re-evaluation, banishing.
When: From two days after the full moon to two days before the new moon.

Winter Tales

Here are various dark comedies, psychological dramas, and related stories for winter (see page 140). Each offering provides an engaging storyline, laughter, and ultimately satisfying resolutions.

Movies & Film

Bad Santa (2003) - A dark comedy about a conman disguised as Santa Claus - unexpected encounters change his perspective.
Eternal Sunshine of the Spotless Mind (2004) - A romantic comedy-drama where a couple tries to erase their memories.
The Long Kiss Goodnight (1996) - Action-comedy about a woman suffering from amnesia who discovers her past as an assassin.
The Ref (1994) - A cat burglar takes a dysfunctional family hostage on Christmas Eve.
The Dead Don't Die (2019) - A zombie comedy featuring a unique blend of humor and social commentary.
Four Rooms (1995) - An anthology comedy.
About Schmidt (2002) - A recently retired man goes on a soul-searching journey, reflecting on his life and relationships.
Winter's Tale (2014) - A romantic fantasy intertwining the stories of a burglar, a dying woman, and a magical white horse.
Christmas Vacation (1989) – The Griswold family's plans go awry, resulting in hilarious mishaps and chaotic situations.
Groundhog Day (1993) - A weatherman relives the same day in a time loop—a good movie to watch between Yule and Imbolc.

Books

The Snow Child by Eowyn Ivey - A novel inspired by a Russian fairytale, following a childless couple who build a snow child that comes to life in the Alaskan wilderness.
A Dirty Job by Christopher Moore - A darkly comedic fantasy novel about a man who becomes a Grim Reaper and must navigate supernatural challenges while dealing with personal losses.
The Stupidest Angel: A Heartwarming Tale of Christmas Terror by Christopher Moore - A comedic tale about a small town where a bumbling angel attempts to grant a child's Christmas wish.
The Hundred-Year-Old Man Who Climbed Out of the Window and Disappeared by Jonas Jonasson - A centenarian escapes his nursing home and embarks on a journey involving criminals, detectives, and unexpected encounters.
Beartown by Fredrik Backman - A story set in a small town obsessed with ice hockey, exploring themes of community, loyalty, and personal growth.

Easy Lotion Recipe

Creating lotions at home is an excellent opportunity to delve into herbs, essential oils, carrier oils, chemistry, and cosmetic formulation. It allows you to choose each ingredient carefully based on availability, potential allergies, cost, and unique healing properties. Moreover, you can infuse your lotion-making process with a touch of magic! Let's explore the art of crafting lotions step by step.

Lotions are created in distinct phases, similar to when you follow a muffin recipe that combines wet and dry ingredients separately before blending them. These phases add complexity to the lotion-making process, primarily due to the need for precise temperature control. The number of phases in a lotion formula can vary depending on the ingredients, but for this quick lotion, we will focus on two phases.

A lotion is an emulsion that combines oil and water. However, this blend creates an environment susceptible to bacteria, fungi, and yeast growth. Since the lotion recipe we'll be working with doesn't contain preservatives, making small batches and using them within two or three weeks is recommended. Alternatively, you can refrigerate the lotion for up to six weeks. Maintaining cleanliness by using clean hands, tools, and containers is crucial to prevent contamination. Furthermore, the oils in the lotion can become rancid when they oxidize, but you can slow down this oxidation process and enjoy some healing benefits by incorporating Vitamin E into your formulas.

Oil and water naturally separate, like oil and vinegar in salad dressing. To prevent separation, an emulsifier is needed to create a creamy consistency. In salad dressings, the emulsifier is often egg yolk. In lotions, emulsifying wax, a combination of Cetearyl alcohol and polysorbate 60, is commonly used. However, we will rely on gelled aloe vera for our lotion to aid in emulsification.

Ingredients for Phase A

- **½ cup of Oil**
  Choose an oil that remains liquid at room temperature. Olive, hemp, jojoba, or rosehip oils work well for dry skin. Almond and apricot oils suit most skin types, while grapeseed oil can benefit oily skin. Creating a blend of different oils totaling ½ cup will result in a more nourishing lotion due to the broader range of fatty acids.

  You can use oils infused with botanicals for an added touch of magic. For instance, infusing your oil with dried rosemary enhances purification and protection, while adding rose petals enhances love, beauty, and confidence. Allow the dried botanicals to sit in the oil for a few weeks in a dark spot, stirring them daily or every other day. Strain out the herbs before using the oil.
- **1 ounce of Beeswax**
- **1 teaspoon Vitamin E Oil**
  Choose a low alpha-tocopherol vitamin E, such as T50 vitamin E. Alternately, you can extract the contents from a few pierced dietary supplement capsules.
- **14 drops Essential Oil**
  Choose a skin-safe essential oil like frankincense, patchouli, lemongrass, clary sage, rosemary, or rose. Use half the amount for peppermint or eucalyptus (7 drops).

Ingredient for Phase B

- **1 cup Aloe Vera Gel**
  Look for thick, jelly-like gel typically found near sunscreen products in stores. It should contain at least 98% pure aloe vera. Thick gels work better than runny ones, so you can check by tipping the bottle in the store to see if any air bubbles travel through the gel too quickly. Small amounts of glycerin or coloring will not adversely affect your lotion if the gel is 98% aloe vera. Using aloe vera from your plant will not work for this specific formula.

Lotion Procedure

Phase A

- Mix ½ cup of oil and beeswax in a large microwave-safe bowl. Heat the mixture in the microwave on high power for one minute, then remove and stir. Repeat this process in 30-second intervals, stirring each time, until all the beeswax has completely melted. Be cautious not to over-heat the mixture, as beeswax melts at around 150°F, and it's best to avoid heating it above 170°F.
- Allow the mixture to cool to approximately 120°F before adding Vitamin E and essential oils. Stir thoroughly to ensure everything is well blended.

Phase B

While waiting for Phase A to cool, place the bottle of aloe vera gel in a bowl filled with warm tap water (around 100°F). Try to bring both Phase A and Phase B to the same temperature, ideally around 75-80°F. If you don't have a thermometer, you can gauge the temperature by feeling the containers. Once both phases are slightly warmer than room temperature and have reached a similar temperature, it's time to blend.

Blending

- Use a standard blender or an immersion blender. Begin blending Phase A using the lowest power setting.
- Gradually add Phase B and continue blending. It is crucial that you add the aloe vera gel slowly to achieve the desired consistency. It should take approximately 5 minutes or more to add the gel. If your lotion reaches the desired consistency before using all the aloe vera gel, you can stop adding more. For best results, use at least half of the aloe vera.
- Turn off the blender and scrape the sides of the container as needed.
- Continue to blend until the lotion has thickened, then continue blending for an additional two minutes.

Store your lotion in an airtight jar. Refrigerated lotion will thicken further and has an extended shelf life.

Pagan Power Bowl

There are two meals I never grow tired of, pizza and fried rice. This recipe is a modified fried rice and constitutes most of my meals. I make it at the beginning of each week, which carries me through until the weekend. It will give you the magical and physical energy to stay strong and is packed with nutrients. Omit any ingredients that aren't available or that you don't like.

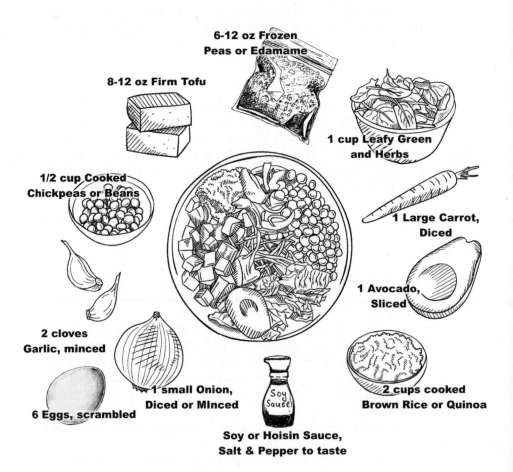

6-12 oz Frozen Peas or Edamame

8-12 oz Firm Tofu

1 cup Leafy Green and Herbs

1/2 cup Cooked Chickpeas or Beans

1 Large Carrot, Diced

1 Avocado, Sliced

2 cloves Garlic, minced

1 small Onion, Diced or Minced

2 cups cooked Brown Rice or Quinoa

6 Eggs, scrambled

Soy or Hoisin Sauce, Salt & Pepper to taste

5-6 Servings   Preparation Time: 20-25 minutes

1. Drain and press tofu. Cut into ½ inch cubes. If you do not like tofu, you can substitute two grilled chicken breasts, diced.
2. Beat and scramble the eggs, then set aside for step seven.
3. In a large pan, saute the minced garlic, onion, and diced carrots in a small amount of vegetable oil. If you substitute garlic powder, add it in step eight. Stir-fry on medium-low heat until the carrots are tender and the onions are golden brown.
4. Add the frozen peas or edamame and continue to heat for a few minutes.
5. Stir in the beans or chickpeas, heat for a few minutes, then stir in the cooked rice or quinoa.
6. Fold in the leafy greens. My favorite blend is a handful of fresh spinach, a handful of kale, and a small bundle of dandelion greens. You can leave your greens whole, but I prefer to chop them coarsely. Continue to cook for a minute or two, stirring gently as needed.
7. Fold in the scrambled eggs.
8. Add the tofu on top of the mixture and sprinkle with seasonings. Start with two tablespoons of soy sauce and adjust to your taste. You can also add salt, pepper, Pad Thai sauce, sesame oil, Hoisin sauce, etc.
9. Gently fold the tofu and seasonings into your blend.
10. Garnish with fresh avocado slices. You may also add fresh herbs such as cilantro, tulsi (holy basil), chives, scallions, green onions, basil, etc.

Storage

Do not store with the avocado garnish. Refrigerate for up to four days or freeze individual portions for easy meals on the go.

Tea Recipes

Purification Tea

- 1 tablespoon of Green Tea (*Camellia sinensis*)
- 1 tablespoon of Lemon Verbena (*Aloysia citriodora*)
- 1 teaspoon of Chamomile (*Matricaria chamomilla*)
- 1 teaspoon of Peppermint (*Mentha x piperita*)

Dreams & Visions Tea

- 1 tablespoon of Chamomile (*Matricaria chamomilla*)
- 1 tablespoon of Lemon Verbena (*Aloysia citriodora*)
- 1 tablespoon of Elderberries (*Sambucus nigra*)
- 1 teaspoon of Mugwort (*Artemisia vulgaris*)

Vitality Tea

- 2 tablespoons of Black Tea (*Camellia sinensis*)
- 1 tablespoon of Hibiscus flowers (*Hibiscus sabdariffa*)
- 1 tablespoon of Elderberries (*Sambucus nigra*)
- 1 tablespoon of Rose Hips (*Rosa canina*)
- 1 teaspoon of Cinnamon bark chips (*Cinnamomum verum*)

Iced Energy Tea

- 2 tablespoons of Black or Green Tea (*Camellia sinensis*)
- 2 tablespoons of Lemon Verbena (*Aloysia citriodora*)
- 1 tablespoon of Hibiscus (*Hibiscus sabdariffa*)

Protection Tea

- 2 teaspoons of Black or Green Tea (*Camellia sinensis*)
- 1 teaspoon of Hibiscus (*Hibiscus sabdariffa*
- 1 teaspoon of Rose Hips (*Rosa canina* and *Rosa rubiginosa*)
- 1 teaspoon of Elderberries (*Sambucus nigra*)
- ½ teaspoon of Chamomile (*Matricaria chamomilla*)
- ½ teaspoon of Cinnamon (*Cinnamomum verum*)

Love Tea

- 2 tablespoons of Assam or other black tea
- 2 teaspoons of Rose Petals (*Rosa spp.*)
- ½ teaspoon of Lavender Flowers (*Lavandula angustifolia*)
- 1 teaspoon of Hibiscus (*Hibiscus sabdariffa*)
- 1 tablespoon of Cacao Nibs (*Theobroma cacao*)
- ½ teaspoon of Damiana (*Turnera diffusa*)

Magical & Psychic Power Tea

- 1 teaspoon of Mugwort (*Artemisia vulgaris*)
- 2 teaspoons of Lemon Balm (*Melissa officinalis*)
- 2 teaspoons of Peppermint (*Mentha x piperita*)
- 1 teaspoon of Elderberries (*Sambucus nigra*)
- ½ teaspoon of Cinnamon (*Cinnamomum verum*)

Calming and Stress Relief Tea

- 2 tablespoons of Chamomile (*Matricaria chamomilla*)
- 1 tablespoon of Lavender (*Lavandula angustifolia*)
- 1 tablespoon of Lemon Balm (*Melissa officinalis*)
- 1 teaspoon of Passionflower (*Passiflora incarnata*)

Friday's Easy Apple Butter

Processing a large apple harvest can be simplified by using this technique to make apple butter. If you don't have a large apple harvest or don't want to peel and chop dozens of apples, you can cheat by starting with unsweetened apple sauce. I use "number ten" cans intended for restaurants or a few large jars from the grocer. If you purchase applesauce, skip the first three steps of these directions.

Do not use sweetened applesauce for this technique. The added sugar will caramelize at a higher temperature than the sugars naturally found in the apples, and raising the oven temperature to compensate will scorch the apple butter.

• Peel and core apples and chop them up into large chunks.

• Fill a slow cooker or crock pot with ¼ inch of water.

• Add the apple chunks and cook until they are soft and begin to break down. Stir and mash occasionally with a potato masher until you have applesauce. This can take two or more hours.

• Pour your applesauce into shallow, non-reactive pans such as jelly roll pans or standard 9x12 cake pans.

• Bake at 230°F for 30-60 minutes, stirring occasionally. Continue baking as necessary until the apples are caramelized, and have achieved a desirable color.

• Allow the pans to cool until you can safely handle them. Pour the caramelized apples into a large bowl and beat with a hand mixer. Add sugar and lemon juice as desired to adjust sweetness and tang.

Moon Sign Magic

Moon Sign	Energy Keywords
♈ Aries	Confidence, New Projects, Energy, Motivation, Justice, Protection, Success, Breakthroughs, Progress
♉ Taurus	Creativity, Sensuality, Romance, Security, Money, Prosperity, Grounding, Property, Gratitude, Growth
♊ Gemini	Relationships, Balance, Harmony, Communication, Mental Powers, Attraction
♋ Cancer	Love, Relationships, Fertility, Family, Creativity, Nurturing, Intuition, Psychic Skills, Divination, Home
♌ Leo	Friendship, Love, Romance, Optimism, Passion, Creativity, Strength, Charisma
♍ Virgo	Purification, Waning, Banishing, Healing, Writing, Organizing, Grounding, Exorcism
♎ Libra	Balance, Beauty, Connecting, Justice, Legal Matters, Marriage, Creativity, Revealing Truth, Partnerships
♏ Scorpio	Exploring Your Shadows, Personal Growth, Change, Sensuality, Passion, Psychic Skills, Divination, Releasing, Protection
♐ Sagittarius	Confidence, Luck, Planning, Divination, Adventure, Fun, Travel, Gambling, Revealing Truth, Career Success
♑ Capricorn	Releasing, Banishing, Productivity, Focus, Bond-Breaking, Reversals, Self-Promotion
♒ Aquarius	Expression, Friendship, Psychic Skills, Meditation, Releasing, Breaking Old Patterns
♓ Pisces	Spirit and Ancestral Contact, Intuition, Divination, Healing, Meditations, Shielding, Obfuscating, Psychic Skills

Name Numerology

Numerology is the study of numbers and their occult significance. It can offer valuable insights into the energetic vibrations and influences surrounding us. Calculating the numerological equivalent of a name can provide a deeper understanding of the inherent qualities and potential associated with it. This also adds a fascinating layer of understanding to the journey of self-discovery and personal growth. Use this guide to calculate the numerological equivalent of a name.

1. Assign numerical values to each letter using the chart below. The name Sara is S1, A1, R9, A1.

2. Add up the numerical values of each letter in the name. Using our same example, Sara is 1 + 1 + 9 + 1= 12.

3. Reduce the total to a single-digit number by adding the individual digits together. Sara is 12, so add 1 plus 2 for a total of 3. This single-digit number (3) represents the numerological equivalent of the name. Research the meaning of your name's number to reveal interesting traits and associations.

Pythagorean Numerology Chart

1	2	3	4	5	6	7	8	9
A	B	C	D	E	F	G	H	I
J	K	L	M	N	O	P	Q	R
S	T	U	V	W	X	Y	Z	

Numerological Meanings

These are general interpretations of the meanings of numbers and can vary based on different numerological systems and personal beliefs. Use the guide on the previous page to determine your name's number.

1 Independence, new beginnings, individuality, self-confidence, leadership, pioneering.

2 Cooperation, balance, harmony, partnerships, diplomacy, unity, adaptability, receptivity.

3 Creativity, self-expression, communication, joy, inspiration, optimism, socializing.

4 Stability, practicality, organization, hard work, structure, discipline, order, steady growth, pragmatic, reliable.

5 Freedom, adventure, versatility, change, adaptability, exploration, unpredictability.

6 Harmony, balance, family, love, responsibility, nurturing, compassion, empathy, service.

7 Introspection, spirituality, inner wisdom, analysis, intuition, introspection.

8 Abundance, success, power, achievement, material gains, ambition, authority.

9 Completion, humanitarianism, spiritual enlightenment, transformation, forgiveness, creative expression, universal love.

Rune Keywords

Fehu /fay-who/
Controlled power over wealth. Manifesting creative energy and power. Invest wisely.

Uruz /oo-rooz/
Primal power, determination health, perseverance, manifestation, wisdom & lore

Thurisaz /thoor-ee-sahs/
Thorn, protection, barrier, enemy of baneful forces, defense, destruction, applied power

Ansuz /ahn-sooz/
Breath, word/song, incantations, shaping power or sound, expression, communication

Raidho /rye-thoh/
Riding, wheel, journey and travel, quest, change, ritual, rhythm, movement, order, the underworld

Kenaz /kane-ahz/
Torch, light, fires of transformation, passion, illumination, regeneration, enlightenment, kinship

Gebo /gay-boh/
Gift, exchange of power, relationships, crossing paths or uniting, connections, balance

Wunjo /woon-yo/
Joy, perfection, shared goals, harmony of like forces, happiness

Hagalaz /haw-gah-lahs/
Hail, hailstone, disruption, destruction, seed form, moving ice, overcome hardship

Naudhiz /now-theez/
Need, necessity, distress, necessity is the mother of invention, resistance, friction→fire

Isa /ee-sah/
Ice, contraction, stillness, suspension, introspection, restraint, slowed growth, stagnation

Jera /yur-ah/
Harvest, year, season, cycle, the flow of life-death-rebirth, fruition, completion, sow/reap

Eihwaz /ii-wahz/ ï (æ)
Yew tree, world axis, endings/beginnings, opportunity, passage, between, protection

Perthro /pear-throh/
Dice cup, vulva, birth, problem-solving, evolutionary force, chance, destiny

Elhaz /ale-hawz/ or /all-geese/
Elk, protection, defense, support, luck, shielding, sanctuary, deity connection

Sowilo /soh-wil-oh/ or /so-woo-loh/
Sun, will, victory, success, vitality, healing, solar energy and movement, directing power, clarity

Tiwaz /tee-wahz/
Creator, justice, success, responsibility, victory, a good path, law & order

Berkano /bear-kahn-oh/
Birch, life-death-rebirth, regeneration, growth, intuition, female fertility, new beginnings

Ehwaz /ay-wahz/ or /ay-woh/ Horse, movement, connections, connecting with another force to achieve a goal

Mannaz /mahn-nahz/
Man (human), exam, dispute, challenge, arguments, gaining upper hand, communication.

Laguz /lah-gooz/
Water, lake, flowing, emotion, intuition, psychic power, revealing what is hidden

Ingwaz /eeng-wahz/ Fertility, Frey, potential energy, opportunity, how endings affect beginnings

Othala /oath-ah-lah/ Home, sacred ancestral land, inherited land, inheritance, ancestral power, true wealth and treasures (rather than currency).

Magical Days of the Week

Day	Keywords	Planet
Monday	New beginnings, balancing emotions, intuition, shadow work, dreams, psychic abilities, introspection	Moon
Tuesday	Legal matters, courage, confidence, action, justice, protection, reversal, passion, banishing, determination	Mars
Wednesday	Reflection, devotion, divination, travel, luck, communication, knowledge, healing, adaptability	Mercury
Thursday	Money, prosperity, cleansing, marriage, luck, growth, oaths, success, influence, expansion, generosity	Jupiter
Friday	Love, romance, passion, beauty, home, family, fertility, art, sexuality, birth and rebirth, harmony, attraction	Venus
Saturday	Banishing, cleansing, meditation, protection, transformation, binding, spirit/ancestor contact, discipline, structure	Saturn
Sunday	Success, growth, protection, inspiration, defense, strength, power, healing, leadership, vitality	Sun

Theban Script

Theban script is a substitution cipher that keeps spells and magical writings private.

A	B	C	D	E	F	G	H
ꝏ	ꝗ	ꟺ	ꟽ	ꝛ	ꝝ	ꝟ	ꝣ
I & J	K	L	M	N	O	P	Q
ꝟ	ꝏ	ꝥ	ꝧ	ꝩ	ꝫ	ꝭ	ꝯ
R	S	T	U & V	W	X	Y	Z
ꝰ	ꝱ	ꝲ	ꝳ	ꝵ	ꝷ	ꝸ	ꝺ

Roman Numerals in Tarot

Reading the Roman numerals from I to XXI in the Major Arcana tarot cards is a fundamental aspect of tarot interpretation. Each numeral represents a specific card in the tarot deck and carries its own unique symbolism.

I represents one, V is five, and X is ten. Doubled letters signify doubling the value (II is two, XX is twenty), while tripled letters signify tripling (III is three, XXX is thirty).

When a lower-value letter is to the left of a higher-value one, you subtract the lower from the greater (IV is 5 - 1 = 4, IX is 10 - 1 = 9). Conversely, when a lower-value letter is on the right of a higher-value one, you add the lower to the greater (VI is 5 + 1 = 6).

O The Fool

The Fool tarot card is unique in the Major Arcana as it is typically numbered with the Arabic numeral 0 (zero) instead of a Roman numeral. By assigning the Fool the number 0, the tarot emphasizes the Fool's role as a catalyst for transformation and the initiation of a new cycle. The 0 serves as a powerful symbol of potential and the blank canvas upon which one's destiny is written.

Tarot Keywords

U=Upright Keywords   R=Reversed Keywords

Major Arcana

0. **0 The Fool**
   U: Spontaneity, New beginnings, Innocence, Courage
   R: Foolishness, Naivety, Carelessness, Recklessness
1. **I The Magician**
   U: Power, Manifestation, Action, Potential
   R: Manipulation, Trickery, Misuse of skills, Lack of direction
2. **II The High Priestess**
   U: Intuition, Wisdom, Divine Feminine, Mystery
   R: Secrets, Lack of clarity, Ignoring intuition, Hidden agendas
3. **III The Empress**
   U: Fertility, Abundance, Nurturing, Creativity
   R: Dependency, Neglect, Overindulgence, Imbalance
4. **IV The Emperor**
   U: Authority, Structure, Leadership, Discipline
   R: Domination, Control issues, Lack of discipline, Tyranny
5. **V The Hierophant**
   U: Tradition, Spiritual guidance, Conformity, Education
   R: Rebellion, Nonconformity, Unorthodox beliefs, Dogmatism
6. **VI The Lovers**
   U: Love, Union, Harmony, Partnerships, Alliances
   R: Disharmony, Choices, Unrequited love, Conflict
7. **VII The Chariot**
   U: Determination, Willpower, Victory, Control, Taking the lead
   R: Lack of control, Directionless, Roadblocks, Others lead
8. **VIII Strength**
   U: Inner strength, Courage, Patience, Resilience
   R: Self-doubt, Weakness, Power struggles, Lack of confidence
9. **IX The Hermit**
   U: Solitude, Reflection, Inner guidance, Wisdom
   R: Isolation, Withdrawal, Loneliness, Self-imposed exile
10. **X Wheel of Fortune**
    U: Change, Destiny, Good luck, Cycles
    R: Bad luck, Stagnation, Lack of control, Unpredictability

Check out the official website for a printable tarot deck and list of keywords! PracticalWitch.com

11. **XI Justice**
    U: Fairness, Balance, Truth, Impartiality
    R: Injustice, Imbalance, Dishonesty, Bias

12. **XII The Hanged Man**
    U: Surrender, Perspective, Letting go, Sacrifice
    R: Resistance, Stagnation, Delays, Idecision

13. **XIII Death**
    U: Transformation, Endings, Renewal, Rebirth
    R: Resistance to change, Stagnation, Fear of loss

14. **XIV Temperance**
    U: Balance, Harmony, Moderation, Adaptability
    R: Imbalance, Extremes, Discord, Lack of self-control

15. **XV The Devil**
    U: Temptation, Addiction, Materialism
    R: Release, Freedom, Overcoming limitations

16. **XVI The Tower**
    U: Sudden change, Chaos, Awakening, Revelation
    R: Avoidance, Delayed disaster, Fear of change

17. **XVII The Star**
    U: Hope, Inspiration, Healing
    R: Lack of faith, Disillusionment, Setbacks

18. **XVIII The Moon**
    U: Intuition, Illusion, Subconscious, Mystery
    R: Confusion, Deception, Anxiety, Irrationality

19. **XIX The Sun**
    U: Vitality, Joy, Success, Positivity
    R: Temporary setbacks, Ego, Overconfidence

20. **XX Judgment**
    U: Rebirth, Awakening, Forgiveness, Redemption
    R: Self-doubt, Regret, Fear of judgment, Ignoring lessons

21. **XXI The World**
    U: Completion, Wholeness, Achievement, Success
    R: Unfinished business, Stagnation, Lack of closure, Limits

Minor Arcana — Wands

Ace of Wands
U: Creative potential, Inspiration, New beginnings R: Blocked energy, Lack of direction, Delays
Two of Wands
U: Planning, Personal power, Future vision R: Lack of planning, Self-doubt, Stagnation
Three of Wands
U: Expansion, Progress, Exploration R: Lack of progress, Setbacks, Limited vision
Four of Wands
U: Celebration, Harmony, Homecoming R: Discord, Disruption, Lack of stability
Five of Wands
U: Conflict, Competition, Energy in motion R: Resolution, Cooperation, Inner conflict
Six of Wands
U: Victory, Recognition, Public acclaim R: Ego, Setbacks, Lack of recognition
Seven of Wands
U: Courage, Perseverance, Standing your ground R: Overwhelm, Defensive, Lack of confidence
Eight of Wands
U: Swiftness, Progress, Action R: Delays, Miscommunication, Lack of momentum
Nine of Wands
U: Resilience, Persistence, Inner strength R: Burnout, Exhaustion, Self-doubt
Ten of Wands
U: Burdens, Responsibility, Overwhelm R: Release, Delegation, Lightening the load
Page of Wands
U: Passion, Enthusiasm, New opportunities R: Impulsiveness, Lack of direction, Restlessness
Knight of Wands
U: Energy, Adventure, Courageous action R: Impatience, Recklessness, Aggression
Queen of Wands
U: Confidence, Creativity, Leadership R: Manipulation, Jealousy, Selfishness
King of Wands
U: Charisma, Authority, Inspiration R: Dictatorship, Arrogance, Abuse of power

Minor Arcana — Cups

Ace of Cups
U: Love, New emotions, Spiritual connection
R: Blocked emotions, Emotional loss, Lack of fulfillment
Two of Cups
U: Union, Partnership, Harmony
R: Imbalance, Disharmony, Broken bonds
Three of Cups
U: Celebration, Friendship, Community
R: Overindulgence, Excessive socializing, Gossip
Four of Cups
U: Contemplation, Reflection, Emotional stability
R: Discontent, Boredom, Missed opportunities
Five of Cups
U: Loss, Grief, Regret
R: Acceptance, Moving on, Finding silver linings
Six of Cups
U: Nostalgia, Innocence, Childhood memories
R: Living in the past, Naivety, Emotional baggage
Seven of Cups
U: Choices, Dreams, Imagination
R: Confusion, Illusion, Lack of focus
Eight of Cups
U: Seeking deeper meaning, Letting go, Soul-searching
R: Fear of change, Clinging to the past, Unresolved issues
Nine of Cups
U: Contentment, Emotional fulfillment, Wishes granted
R: Self-indulgence, Greed, Unfulfilled desires
Ten of Cups
U: Harmony, Joy, Family happiness
R: Disharmony, Broken family ties, Unrealistic expectations
Page of Cups
U: Emotional messages, Creativity, Intuition
R: Emotional immaturity, Unrealistic fantasies, Moodiness
Knight of Cups
U: Romantic pursuit, Passion, Emotional adventure
R: Emotional manipulation, Mood swings, Impulsiveness
Queen of Cups
U: Emotional maturity, Nurturing, Intuition
R: Emotional manipulation, Co-dependency, Over-sensitivity
King of Cups
U: Emotional stability, Compassion, Wisdom
R: Emotional volatility, Manipulation, Hidden agendas

Minor Arcana — Swords

Ace of Swords
U: Mental clarity, New ideas, Breakthroughs R: Confusion, Mental blockage, Miscommunication

Two of Swords
U: Difficult decisions, Balance, Indecision R: Stalemate, Avoidance, Inner conflict

Three of Swords
U: Heartbreak, Grief, Betrayal R: Healing, Forgiveness, Release of pain

Four of Swords
U: Rest, Retreat, Reflection R: Restlessness, Burnout, Lack of downtime

Five of Swords
U: Conflict, Dishonesty, Winning at all costs R: Resolution, Compromise, Moving on from conflict

Six of Swords
U: Transition, Healing, Moving forward R: Resistance to change, Unresolved issues, Stagnation

Seven of Swords
U: Deception, Stealth, Strategy R: Guilt, Confession, Consequences

Eight of Swords
U: Feeling trapped, Self-imposed limitations, Fear R: Liberation, Breaking free, Empowerment

Nine of Swords
U: Anxiety, Nightmares, Inner turmoil R: Release of fear, Healing, Peace of mind

Ten of Swords
U: Rock bottom, Endings, Transformation R: Recovery, Resilience, Moving on

Page of Swords
U: Curiosity, Intellect, Communication R: Gossip, Dishonesty, Misuse of power

Knight of Swords
U: Action, Ambition, Determination R: Aggression, Impulsiveness, Recklessness

Queen of Swords
U: Clarity, Independence, Wisdom R: Coldness, Harsh judgment, Isolation

King of Swords
U: Mental strength, Authority, Strategic thinking R: Manipulation, Tyranny, Abuse of power

Minor Arcana — Pentacles

Ace of Pentacles
U: Material abundance, Prosperity, New opportunities R: Financial instability, Lost opportunities, Lack of abundance

Two of Pentacles
U: Balance, Adaptability, Time management R: Imbalance, Over-commitment, Poor planning

Three of Pentacles
U: Collaboration, Skill mastery, Teamwork R: Lack of teamwork, Mediocrity, Miscommunication

Four of Pentacles
U: Financial stability, Security, Conservation R: Greed, Financial insecurity, Fear of loss

Five of Pentacles
U: Financial hardship, Isolation, Material loss R: Recovery, Support, Hope

Six of Pentacles
U: Generosity, Charity, Prosperity shared R: Greed, Selfishness, Financial imbalance

Seven of Pentacles
U: Patience, Investment, Long-term growth R: Impatience, Lack of progress, Unfulfilled potential

Eight of Pentacles
U: Skill development, Dedication, Craftsmanship R: Lack of focus, Mediocrity, Skill stagnation

Nine of Pentacles
U: Abundance, Self-sufficiency, Luxury R: Dependency, Financial loss, Isolation

Ten of Pentacles
U: Wealth, Legacy, Family security R: Financial instability, Family discord, Lost inheritance

Page of Pentacles
U: Manifestation, Opportunity, Practicality R: Lack of ambition, Missed opportunities, Lack of focus

Knight of Pentacles
U: Responsibility, Reliability, Hard work R: Laziness, Stubbornness, Lack of progress

Queen of Pentacles
U: Nurturing, Abundance, Practicality R: Materialism, Financial dependence, Indulgence

King of Pentacles
U: Financial security, Business acumen, Leadership R: Greed, Financial setbacks, Misuse of finances

Color Magic

Color	Magical & Metaphysical Correspondences	Hexadecimal & RGB
Red	Passion, Energy, Action, Courage, Love	#FF0000 255, 0, 0
Pink	Love, Friendship, Beauty, Romance, Compassion, Gentleness	#FFC0CB 255, 192, 203
Orange	Creativity, Joy, Abundance, Success	#FFA500 255, 165, 0
Yellow	Happiness, Intellect, Optimism, Clarity	#FFFF00 255, 255, 0
Green	Growth, Renewal, Healing, Prosperity	#008000 0, 128, 0
Light Blue	Calmness, Serenity, Communication, Harmony, Healing, Peace	#ADD8E6 173, 216, 230
Dark Blue	Wisdom, Intuition, Spirituality, Depth, Psychic Skills	#00008B 0, 0, 139
Indigo	Psychic Abilities, Perception, Divine Connection	#4B0082 75, 0, 130
Purple	Spirituality, Magic, Transformation, Royalty, Psychic Powers	#800080 128, 0, 128
Violet	Imagination, Spirit Communication, Inspiration, Psychic Powers	#EE82EE 238, 130, 238
Black	Protection, Mystery, Banishing, Grounding, Reversals	#000000 0, 0, 0
Gray	Neutrality, Balance, Wisdom, Shielding, Practicality	#808080 128, 128, 128
White	Purity, Spiritual Enlightenment, Clarity, Healing	#FFFFFF 255, 255, 255
Brown	Stability, Grounding, Connection to Nature, Earth energy	#A52A2A 165, 42, 42
Silver	Intuition, Reflection, Lunar Energies, Clairvoyance, The Moon	#C0C0C0 192, 192, 192
Gold	Abundance, Wealth, Success, Higher Self, The Sun	#FFD700 255, 215, 0

Using the Quick Guides

Magical correspondences are symbolic associations between various components (colors, herbs, crystals, etc.) and specific intentions or energies. Witches use correspondences in sympathetic magic to tap into the energies of each component, harnessing their power to amplify and focus intention.

The Practical Witch's Almanac is taking a new approach to magical correspondences. For almost forty years, I have observed that we witches focus on eight primary types of rituals and spellwork. Most of us need a quick reference when designing our workings, precisely what this section offers.

The correspondences provided for eight areas of focus include plants and stones. I've sprinkled some invocations in a few places to use when casting spells. Feel free to adapt the words in these invocations to suit your needs and preferences.

Regardless of its correspondences, use the stone you are intuitively drawn to. Each stone possesses distinct characteristics, making it crucial to select the one that resonates with you and aligns with your intentions.

It is essential to regularly cleanse and recharge your stones to ensure they maintain their optimal energetic properties. Instead of discarding stones after use, consider cleansing and recharging them so you can reuse them in other spells and rituals.

Use caution when a plant name is preceded with the skull and crossbones (☠). These toxic plants should not be used in incense or consumed. They can be used with caution in spell bottles and bags. Always research any plant before ingesting.

Protection

Use these components to ward off baneful energies and harmful influences. They are effective in countering curses or hexes and psychic or spiritual attacks.

Stones, Crystals & Minerals

Amethyst, Black Tourmaline, Bloodstone, Blue Lace Agate, Carnelian, Charoite, Clear Quartz, Fluorite, Hematite, Jasper, Labradorite, Lapis Lazuli, Malachite, Moonstone, Obsidian, Onyx, Pyrite, Rhodonite, Rose Quartz, Ruby, Selenite, Serpentine, Shungite, Smoky Quartz, Snowflake Obsidian, Sodalite, Tiger's Eye, Tourmalinated Quartz, Turquoise, Unakite

Herbs & Plants

Angelica, Basil, Bay leaves, Cedar, Cinnamon, Clove, Dill, Dragon's blood, Eucalyptus, Elder, Frankincense, Garlic, Heather, Hyssop, Juniper, Lavender, Lemon balm, Mugwort, Myrrh, Nettle, Palo Santo, Patchouli, Peppermint, Rosemary, Rue, Sage, Sandalwood, St. John's Wort, Thyme, Valerian

Invocation

By Earth, Air, Fire, and Sea,
I invoke protection, so mote it be.
Shield me now, both night and day,
Keeping bane and harm away.

 # Love & Attraction

Use these components to attract love, friendship, and self-confidence. They also enhance existing relationships, overcome self-doubt, and promote effective communication.

Stones, Crystals & Minerals

Amethyst, Carnelian, Emerald, Garnet, Jade, Lapis Lazuli, Moonstone, Opal, Pearl, Pink Tourmaline, Rhodonite, Rose Quartz, Ruby, Sapphire, Smoky Quartz, Sugilite, Sunstone, Tanzanite, Topaz, Turquoise

Herbs & Plants

Apple, Basil, Cardamom, Chamomile, Cinnamon, Clove, Damiana, Ginger, Hibiscus, Jasmine, Lavender, Lemon balm, Lilac, Marjoram, Mint, Orange, Patchouli, Peony, Rose, Rosemary, Sandalwood, Strawberry, Thyme, Vanilla, Vervain, Violet, Yarrow, Ylang-ylang

Invocation

With free-will and intentions pure,
I call upon love to now endure.
By love's gentle might, I cast my plea,
To attract true love, yet honor each free.
With open hearts, our paths align,
Love's embrace, let it be mine.

Ancestral Work

These components facilitate ancestral connections when you seek guidance, healing, and wisdom; or to establish stronger bonds with ancestral lineage.

Stones, Crystals & Minerals

Amethyst, Apache Tear, Bloodstone, Carnelian, Charoite, Clear Quartz, Fossils, Labradorite, Lepidolite, Moldavite, Moonstone, Obsidian, Petrified Wood, Rhodonite, Rose Quartz, Selenite, Smoky Quartz, Sodalite, Tiger's Eye, Tree Agate, Unakite

Herbs & Plants

Angelica Root, Bay Leaf,
Calendula, Cedar,
Chamomile, Dandelion,
Eucalyptus, Frankincense,
Juniper, Lavender,
Mugwort, Mushrooms,
Myrrh, Palo Santo,
Patchouli, Rosemary, Rue,
Sage, White Sage,
Wormwood, Yarrow

Invocation

Ancestors wise, spirits of old,
In this sacred space, let your presence unfold.
With open heart, I call upon thee,
Guidance and wisdom, I humbly plea.
From the depths of time, across the veil,
Join me now, let your presence prevail.

Healing

These are materials used for promoting physical, physical, emotional, or spiritual healing; restoring balance, and improving overall well-being.

Stones, Crystals & Minerals

Amethyst, Black Tourmaline, Carnelian, Clear Quartz, Fluorite, Hematite, Jade, Labradorite, Lapis Lazuli, Malachite, Moonstone, Obsidian, Rose Quartz, Selenite, Smoky Quartz, Sodalite, Tiger's Eye, Turquoise, Unakite, Yellow Jasper

Herbs & Plants

Chamomile, Cinnamon, Eucalyptus, Frankincense, Ginger, Lavender, Lemon Balm, Mugwort, Nettle, Patchouli, Peppermint, Rosemary, Sage, St. John's Wort, Thyme, Valerian, Vervain, White Willow Bark, Yarrow, Ylang-Ylang

Invocation

Restore balance, bring forth peace,
Release all pain, let healing increase.
With open heart, I embrace the flow,
Body, mind, and spirit, made whole.
Through the power that lies within,
Healing energy, will now begin.

Purification & Banishing

Use these components for cleansing spaces, individuals, or objects from baneful energies. These items are also helpful in cutting ties with toxic people and situations and clearing out stagnant energy.

Stones, Crystals & Minerals

Amethyst, Angelite, Apache Tear, Black Onyx, Black Tourmaline, Blue Lace Agate, Carnelian, Celestite, Citrine, Clear Quartz, Fluorite, Howlite, Labradorite, Lepidolite, Moonstone, Rose Quartz, Shungite, Selenite, Smoky Quartz, Snowflake Obsidian

Herbs & Plants

Basil, Cedar, Chamomile, Eucalyptus, Frankincense, Hyssop, Juniper, Lavender, Lemon Balm, Mugwort, Myrrh, Palo Santo, Peppermint, Rosemary, Rue, Sage, Thyme, White Sage, White Willow Bark, Yarrow

General Invocation

Through sacred flame and mystic rhyme,
I banish bane in this space and time.
I purify this space with cleansing might,
Negative energies now take flight.

Invocation For Smoke Cleansing

With smoke and flame, I cleanse this space,
Negative energy I now erase.
As sacred smoke fills the air,
Energy flows, banishing bane and fear.

Shadow Work, Dreams, Visions & Divination

These components aid in gaining insight, guidance, and clarity. They are used to help delve into your unconscious mind, confront repressed aspects of yourself, and heal past wounds.

Stones, Crystals & Minerals

Amethyst, Aquamarine, Black Obsidian, Black Tourmaline, Blue Kyanite, Celestite, Charoite, Hematite, Labradorite, Lapis Lazuli, Moonstone, Obsidian, Onyx, Opal, Rhodochrosite, Rhodonite, Rose Quartz, Selenite, Smoky Quartz, Snowflake Obsidian, Sugilite, Tiger Eye

Herbs & Plants

Angelica, Blue Lotus, Calamus, Damiana, ☠ Henbane, Honeysuckle, Lavender, ☠ Mandrake, Mugwort, Patchouli, Passionflower, Rosemary, Rue, Sage, Skullcap, St. John's Wort, Valerian, Vervain, Wormwood, Yarrow

Invocation

In the depths of darkness, I call upon light,
To illuminate my shadows, with courage and might.
Unveil repressed truths, let healing unfold,
Embrace the shadows, their wisdom untold.
Guide me through shadows, grant strength to explore,
Integrate and transform, like never before.
With gratitude and love, I face what's concealed,
Shadow work begins, my true self revealed.
In divine embrace, I reclaim my true worth,
I invoke the power of shadow, to bring forth rebirth.

Spiritual Connection & Enlightenment

These components deepen spiritual connections, expand consciousness, and help connect with deities and the higher self.

Stones, Crystals & Minerals

Ametrine, Amethyst, Angelite, Apophyllite, Celestite, Charoite, Clear Quartz, Danburite, Iolite, Kyanite, Labradorite, Lapis Lazuli, Larimar, Moldavite, Moonstone, Prehnite, Rhodochrosite, Rhodonite, Selenite, Seraphinite, Sugilite

Herbs & Plants

Angelica, Bay Laurel, Calendula, Chamomile, Frankincense, Lavender, Lemon Balm, Lemongrass, Mugwort, Myrrh, Palo Santo, Patchouli, Rose, Rosemary, Sage, Sandalwood, St. John's Wort, Thyme, Valerian, Vetiver, White Sage, Yarrow, Ylang-Ylang

Invocation

After reciting the invocation, repeat the name of your patron Goddess three times.

Goddess of ancient wisdom, hear my plea,
Guide me to the truth that sets me free.
In your divine embrace, I seek insight,
Unveil the mysteries, show me the light.
Connect me with the depths of my soul,
Reveal the path that makes me whole.
Goddess of magic, love, and divine power,
Awaken the higher self within me this hour.
With reverence and trust, I call your name,
Together we soar, forever we remain.

Luck, Money, & Prosperity

Use these components to attract abundance, luck, wealth, success, and financial opportunities. They help to open doors and ensure a fair outcome in legal matters.

Stones, Crystals & Minerals

Aventurine, Bloodstone, Carnelian, Citrine, Emerald, Fluorite, Garnet, Green Jade, Green Moss Agate, Green Tourmaline, Labradorite, Malachite, Moonstone, Opal, Peridot, Pyrite, Red Jasper, Ruby, Tiger's Eye, Topaz, Unakite, Variscite, Yellow Jasper, Yellow Apatite, Yellow Calcite, and Zircon

Herbs & Plants

Alfalfa, Basil, Carnation, Chamomile, Cinnamon, Clover, Comfrey, Ginger, Green Aventurine, Honeysuckle, Irish Moss, Jasmine, Mint, Patchouli, Peppermint, Rosemary, Thyme, Tonka Bean, Vetiver, Violet, Wealthy Way, and Yellow Dock

Invocation for Money & Prosperity

Wealth and riches, come to me,
Flow abundantly, set me free.
With open heart and open mind,
Financial blessings, now I find.
Money and prosperity, I manifest,
In harmony and abundance, I am blessed.

Invocation for Luck & Success

Blessings of luck, upon me shine,
In every endeavor, victory is mine.
With power and strength, come to me.
This is my will, so mote it be!

Glossary

Bane and Baneful

Bane is anything with an undesirable, contrary, or negative influence. It is a very relative term! Something can be baneful to certain people or in certain situations, while being a blessing for others or under different circumstances. Baneful magic is sometimes called black magic, however this dichotomy of good/evil – black/white – right/wrong, does not properly apply to magic and witchcraft as we tend to look beyond overly simplified and limiting binaries.

Besom

Pronounced bee-zum or bi-zəm, a besom is a broom, specifically a witch's broom that is used ritually to cleanse areas, for fertility rituals, and for handfasting. Handfasting rituals often involve "jumping the broom" and the bonded parties will jump over a besom to symbolize leaving their pasts behind and being united as they move forward into a new life.

Black Moon

There are three types of black moons. *1. A seasonal black moon* is the third new moon of an astronomical season in which there are four new moons. An astrological season is the time period between the quarter Sabbats (solstices and equinoxes). *2. A monthly black moon* is the second new moon in a calendar month with two new moons. *3. A February black moon* occurs about once every nineteen years. This is when there is either no full or no new moon during the month of February. Time zone differences mean that this last type of black moon is not necessarily a worldwide event.

Blue Moon

There are two types of blue moons. *1. A seasonal blue moon* is the third full Moon of an astronomical season in which there are four full Moons. An astrological season is the time period between the quarter Sabbats (solstices and equinoxes). *2. A monthly blue moon* is the second full Moon in a calendar month with two full moons.

Cast Lots or Draw Lots

Casting lots refers to making a random selection. When cards are used it is usually referred to as drawing lots, a form of cartomancy. When runes, bones, shells, grain, coins, or other tools of cleromancy are used it is normally referred to as casting lots.

Cense & Censing

A very old term for smoke-cleansing, meaning to perfume with incense, or to infuse something with incense smoke. This term is preferred over the culturally appropriated word *smudging*.

Censer

An incense burner or thurible.

Divination

Gaining insight through spiritual means such as scrying, tarot cards, runes, tea leaves, or other methods.

Esbat

A ritual held on full moons, sometimes also on new moons.

Exact Cross-Quarters

The precise half-way point between a solstice and an equinox as measured along the ecliptic. Also known as Astronomical Cross-Quarters.

Handfasting

A type of bonding ritual somewhat similar to a marriage. The spiritual bond is agreed upon by all parties involved, and often includes a set time period. Many choose to handfast for "a year and a day". When that period of time comes to an end, those involved review the relationship and decide to either renew their handfasting or go their separate ways. Hand-fasting can also be "until death do us part" or "for now and all of eternity".

Manifest and Manifestation

Made popular by the book and film *The Secret*, these terms are commonly used in reference to the focusing of one's thoughts upon a desired outcome. Witches have adopted the term as a way to quickly express the focusing of our energy, will, and intent to create change in the physical world or within ourselves. Manifestation can also refer to spiritual forms or entities appearing in the physical world, however in this instance the term materialization is better suited.

Micro Moon

A new or full Moon that occurs during apogee. The moon is farther away and may appear smaller.

So mote it be

Frequently incorporated into words of power or used at the end of a spell to "seal and send". It means *let it be so, so shall it be*, or *it is so*.

Super Moon

A new or full Moon that occurs during perigee. The Moon is close to earth and may appear larger and brighter.

Void of Course (Moon)

Void of course times indicate periods when the Moon is not forming any major aspects with other planets before leaving its current sign and entering into a new sign. These times are often considered less favorable for initiating new projects or making important decisions.

Time Zone Conversion

Your almanac is fitted to Central Time and Daylight Saving Time (DST) is accounted for when in effect. Add or subtract hours as indicated for your area.

Auckland, New Zealand +19

New Plymouth, NZ +19

Sydney, Australia +17

Melbourne, Australia +17

Cairns, Australia +16

Adelaide, Australia +16.5

Alice Springs, Australia +15.5

Tokyo, Japan +15

Perth, Australia +14

Shanghai, China +14

Hong Kong, Hong Kong +14

New Delhi, India +11.5

Moscow, Russia +9

Cairo, Egypt +8

Athens, Greece +8

Rovaniemi, Finland +8

Paris, France +7

Longyearbyen, Norway +7

Zürich, Switzerland +7

Berlin, Germany +7

Amsterdam, Netherlands +7

Madrid, Spain +7

Rome, Italy +7

Dublin, Ireland +6

Lisbon, Portugal +6

Prague, Czech Republic +6

Reykjavik, Iceland +6

Glasgow, United Kingdom +6

Ittoqqortoormiit, Greenland +5

Nuuk, Greenland +3

Halifax, Canada +2

Bridgetown, Barbados +2

Nassau, Bahamas +1

Ottawa, Canada +1

Port-au-Prince, Haiti +1

New York, NY, USA +1

Denver, CO, USA -1

Portland, OR, USA -2

Phoenix, AZ, USA -1

Honolulu, HI, USA -4

Hawaii, Puerto Rico, Guam, US Virgin Islands, and most of Arizona (except the Navajo Nation and parts of the north-east corner of the state) do not observe DST. For these or any areas without DST, subtract an hour (-1) from the time provided in your almanac from March 12 to November 5.

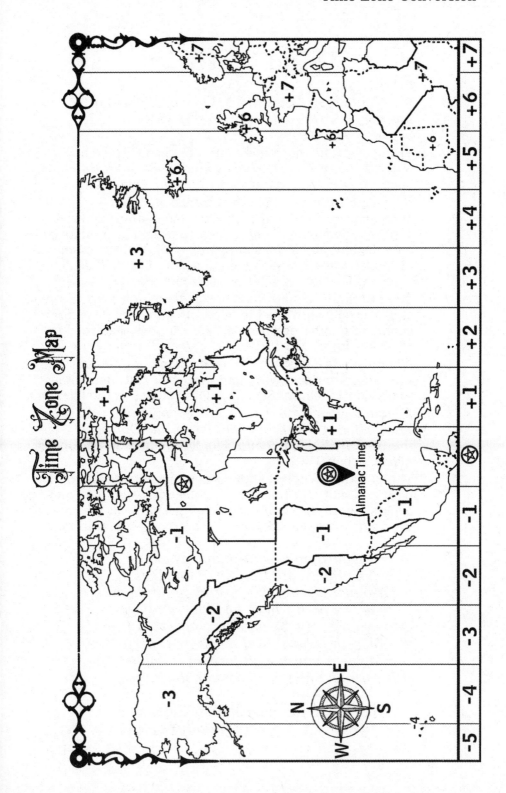

End Notes

1. Illustration: "Hecate" from *Manual of Mythology* by Murray, A. S. (Alexander Stuart), 1898 New York : Scribner, Armstrong

2. Tisane is pronounced much like "tea is on" spoken quickly (tĭ-zăn′, -zän′). Tisanes are blends of herbs and spices that do not contain tea (*Camellia sinensis*).

3. Flashpoint refers to the temperature at which a substance can ignite or produce a flammable vapor when exposed to an open flame or heat source. Flashpoints can vary depending on the source and quality of the essential oil, so it's always a good idea to verify specific flashpoint values with your supplier or manufacturer.

4. The *I Ching* is an ancient Chinese divination text. Yarrow stalks or coins are used to generate numbers. The corresponding numbered entry in the *I Ching* is then read to reveal insights.

5. Aventurine is a durable, food-safe stone but not all stones are safe for contact with food, water, or salt. Remember to do your research if you are using stones in the kitchen.

6. Illustration from *A Smaller Classical Mythology: With Translations from the Ancient Poets, and Questions Upon the Work by William Smith*. London: John Murray, Albemarle Street. 1882. P.85

7. The Practical Witch sanctuary is in the very center of the path of totality for the April 2024 eclipse. Camping and events for witches and Pagans are available at the sanctuary. Visit ArkansasEclipse.org for more information.

Onward now, your magic awakes,
A radiant path that none forsakes.
Through moonlit nights and sunlit days,
Walk the path where enchantment lays.
May your spells be potent, your spirit free,
Blessings bestowed on your sorcery.
May your spirit soar, forever untamed,
Blessings upon your powers unchained.

Thank you for choosing my almanac!
~Friday Gladheart

SUBSCRIBE!

For as little as $15/month, you can support
a small, independent publisher and get
every book that we publish—delivered to
your doorstep!

www.Microcosm.Pub/BFF

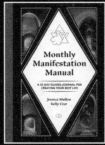